D1361634

HOW CAN I HELP?

W. H. SKIP HUNT

THOMAS NELSON PUBLISHERS

Nashville

The examples and dialogues presented in this book are not those of particular individuals. No case example is that of an actual person. This is necessary to preserve the confidentiality of those who turn to us for help. The events and emotions described in these created cases are, however, representative of the types of situations dealt with on a daily basis on crisis helplines, in counselors' offices, in pastors' studies, and across the kitchen table. The created composites are realistic and true examples of the attitudes and situations that counselors, pastors, and helping friends will confront in today's society. They are, therefore, a good teaching tool for this work.

Published in Nashville, Tennessee, by Thomas Nelson, Inc., Publishers, and distributed in Canada by Word Communications, Ltd., Richmond, British Columbia, and in the United Kingdom by Word (UK), Ltd., Milton Keynes, England.

ISBN 0-7852-8203-3

Printed in the United States of America

1 2 3 4 5 6 — 99 98 97 96 95 94

This book is dedicated
to my dear wife, Anne,
who has labored beside me
in the many rewrites of this book
and in the many years of ministry
together as God has developed
the Christian Helpline ministry through us.

How Can I Help? is an official training program of Christian Helplines, Inc., the association of Christian crisis helplines headquartered in Tampa, Florida. It is the mission of CHI

- To train Christian laypeople to counsel and minister, following the example of Jesus Christ and the teaching of His Holy Bible;

- To provide Christian counseling services through a network of local crisis centers; and . . .

- To share the love of God, His plan of forgiveness and salvation through Jesus Christ, and the transforming power of His Holy Spirit with all who would receive Him, without imposing religious beliefs on anyone.

Letter from President George Bush

In a letter to Christian Helplines, President George Bush said

"Your organization's telephone counseling and crisis intervention programs exemplify the finest spirit of voluntary community service. By reaching out to help your neighbors in their hour of greatest need, you carry on the great American tradition of neighbor helping neighbor. Guided by the teachings of Scripture, you provide counseling and crisis intervention as a Christian response to human suffering. I commend you for providing such an inspiring model of good citizenship and love for your fellowman."

CHRISTIAN HELPLINES
INTERNATIONAL

Contents

Personal Counseling

"Praise be to the God and Father of our Lord Jesus Christ,
the Father of compassion and the God of all comfort,
who comforts us in all our troubles,
so that we can comfort those in any trouble
with the comfort we ourselves have received from God."

2 Corinthians 1:3–4 (NIV)

Chapter 1

How Can I Help?

The telephone rang as I walked down the hall, and I stopped to answer it. I heard my friend's voice at the other end of the line, and I knew something was wrong.

"Martha wants a divorce," he said weakly.

For the next hour, from a thousand miles away, I listened and comforted my friend.

A few days later, I called my mother long-distance to ask her to do a favor for me. As we talked she suddenly began to cry. My counseling experience told me not to try to stop her from crying or ask her a lot of questions. Instead, I waited. I let her cry. When she stopped, I said, "Mom, I love you. Tell me what's wrong."

"I didn't want to worry you," she said. "But I'm going to have surgery on Thursday. It's cancer."

Fortunately, I was able to go and be with her. Family members, friends, and neighbors rallied together, offering prayerful support and quiet conversation. The surgery was a success, for which we were most grateful.

HOW CAN I HELP?

All around us people are hurting and struggling. Divorce, disease, abortion, adultery, depression, loneliness, unemployment: the problems can be overwhelming. We want to reach out and help when we see someone in need. But it's hard to know what to do or say.

The purpose of *How Can I Help?* is to prepare you for those times of crisis when you are called upon for understanding and counsel. Christian Helplines, Inc., the national network of Christian crisis helplines, headquartered in Tampa, Florida, has used *How Can I Help?* to train thousands of laypeople around the world in the basic principles and techniques of personal counseling and evangelism. Those trained have gone on to use their new skills as volunteers in their churches and in various parachurch ministries. Crisis pregnancy centers, prison ministries, telephone helplines, and street ministries use *How Can I Help?* to train staff and volunteers.

Learning to listen and counsel with friends is a challenge. It requires that we learn new communication skills, new ways of thinking. But in the end, it is worth it because it enables us to help those we love the most, friends like Diana.

Jerry and Diana

Jerry and Diana had been married for twenty-four years when Jerry suddenly announced he wanted a divorce. Jerry was excited. He had a girlfriend and a good job. He knew where he was going. He had it all thought out. He was taking scuba lessons and was planning a trip to the islands.

Diana was devastated. She had raised two children. She was hoping she could begin to travel with Jerry. She knew that she and Jerry had problems—they had been to a marriage counselor. But the announced divorce came as a complete surprise.

Diana didn't have a career or a job. She had dropped out of school when she had gotten married. Now she was alone in an empty house, with mortgage payments and no job experience, and emotionally wiped out.

In the depth of her despair Diana reached out and met Jesus. Jesus gave her the love, peace, patience, faith, self-control, plan, and purpose that she needed in her life.

Diana got a job in a department store, discovered she had a gift for retailing, finished her degree at a local college, met Bob, got married, and sold her house. She and Bob now live at the lake, own a marina, and love it. The grandchildren all want to come every weekend.

Jerry got a sunburn in Aruba and spent all his money trying to be as young as his girlfriend. And she left him.

Jerry has been wearing gold chains and open shirts ever since. He has found no genuine relationships. Outside he has a tan and a big smile, but inside he's crying.

It doesn't always happen like this. Jerry could have ended up with the marina and the lake place. Diana might have sold her big house and lived ever after in a small apartment, alone with Jesus. In the eyes of the world Jerry would have been the big winner, but as Christians we know better.

Strange, but so often people must fall into the darkness before they can see the light. So many victims of crisis find the hand of Jesus in the darkness of their struggle. Diana met Jesus in the crisis of her divorce. She now prays that Jerry will come to know Him.

CRISIS: FOR BETTER OR WORSE

Crisis means change. For a person in crisis, the change is often unwanted. But as He did with Diana, God can work within the crisis to bring about good.

Webster defines *crisis* as a "decisive or critical moment, a sudden change for better or worse." The Chinese recognize the possibility of a crisis turning out for better or worse by spelling the word with the two symbols that follow. The symbol at the left means "danger." The symbol at the right means "opportunity." Together the symbols show that, within every crisis exist elements of danger and unique opportunities for growth and development.

 机

When we take the role of helping friends or counselors, we walk with people through the dangers of crisis to the opportunities that lie ahead. Their crises vary in nature, but the stages they must go through in order to experience growth and development are the same: shock, adjustment, and recovery.

Shock

When a crisis first occurs, a person goes into shock. Overwhelmed by an event, the person is temporarily unable to function.

> **Denial:** "This is not really happening."
> **Numbness:** "I can't feel anything."
> **Confusion:** "I don't know what to do."
> **Anger:** "How could he do this to me?!"
> **Guilt:** "If only I hadn't . . ."
> **Uncertainty:** "What am I going to do?"
> **Fear:** "I won't be able to . . ."
> **Rejection:** "He just left me."

A person in shock typically withdraws. He or she may be unable to cope with minor problems. Friends and family may have to gather to intervene and take care of physical needs.

Adjustment

During the adjustment stage, the person in crisis will experience emotional highs and lows. He or she may struggle to overcome depression, anger, rage, fear, self-pity, or doubt, as well as various physical problems. The person's ability to think clearly may still be impaired. His judgment may not be sound. Therefore, it is usually best for him to continue to delay significant decisions until this phase is past. Gradually, he will adjust, regain hope, and make plans to move forward. At this point, he enters recovery.

Recovery

Recovery is a process, a time of gradually getting better. Recovery begins when hope returns and the person begins to make some progress. The helping friend continues to play a critical role in this stage because even now, the person in crisis is vulnerable. The "victim" of a divorce may negotiate a poor settlement because he or she is anxious to end the nightmare. Business owners, depressed over their business failure, may be taken advantage of.

Each person goes through these stages of crisis at a different pace. The period of shock may last several days for some; a number of weeks for others. Some people may spend weeks adjusting to and recovering from a crisis; others may take months. The chart on the following page shows what this process looks like.

No matter how long it takes, we need to help our friends walk through these stages and return to a normal or even higher level of coping with life. Understanding what causes crisis and the various responses we can give will help us to do that.

WHAT CAUSES CRISIS?

Crisis can often be associated with a significant change in a person's life. Some of these changes occur quickly and without

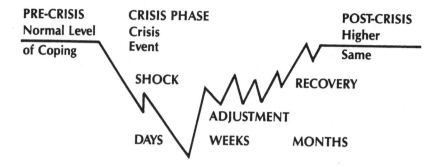

PRE-CRISIS
Normal Level
of Coping

CRISIS PHASE
Crisis
Event

POST-CRISIS
Higher
Same

SHOCK

RECOVERY

ADJUSTMENT

DAYS   WEEKS   MONTHS

warning. This is known as an "accidental crisis." A man suddenly announces he is leaving his wife, a woman is told she has cancer, a friend has a heart attack. These sudden changes throw a person into crisis. We cannot prepare for such events.

A crisis caused by normal anticipated changes is called a "developmental crisis." Graduation, marriage, a move to a new city, retirement: these are all planned events that are part of everyday living. Yet, the changes from these events can be so significant that a crisis results. Whether a crisis occurs or not depends on how a person perceives the change and how he responds.

An "actual" or "potential" crisis is the result of an actual event, or a potential or imagined threat. A woman may lose her job. Or, she may simply fear losing her job because of the economy. Whether the threat is imagined or real, the fear can cause a crisis.

When a number of minor problems are triggered by one major event, a "compound crisis" occurs. A man may lose his job, which in turn leaves him unable to pay his bills. This can lead to his being evicted from his apartment. At this point, his car may just happen to need repairing. When it rains, it pours. His termination has resulted in a compound crisis.

Some people are in a continual state of crisis. This is called "chronic crisis." When people refuse to deal with their problems, even after intense therapy, or have chronic mental or emotional problems, they live in a state of chronic crisis.

Your response to people in crisis will depend upon their emotional state and what stage they are in when they come to see you. Some people will need a friend to take control; they'll need you to help them make plans, be directive. At other times, people will need love and reassurance; they may simply need someone to listen while they evaluate their situation and make decisions about their future. In the first case, crisis intervention is necessary; in the latter, crisis counseling.

Crisis Intervention

After five years of dating seriously, Ted and Susie became engaged. Two months later, Ted broke it off, saying he just didn't feel right about the relationship.

Devastated, Susie swallowed a bottle of sleeping pills and everything else she could find in the medicine cabinet. When her stomach began to cramp, she suddenly became afraid. So she called our helpline. The telephone counselor intervened, summoned the emergency medical service, and Susie's life was saved.

Crisis intervention deals with an immediate threat or event. When a situation is violent, critical, or, as with Susie, life-threatening, crisis intervention is necessary. Crisis intervention is directive action; that is, you must take control because the person in crisis is unable to function. He can no longer cope or adequately respond. People needing crisis intervention include battered wives, abused children, people needing medical attention, people who are suicidal or threatening to hurt others.

Crisis Counseling

If Susie had not taken the pills, but instead, had called the crisis helpline, crisis counseling would have been the more appropriate action. A nondirective approach, crisis counseling helps people to better understand their feelings, problems, resources, and alternatives for developing a plan of action. The crisis counselor guides and directs by presenting ideas the counselee can consider and choose to act upon. The problem is, after all, the counselee's. When your conversation is over, he will have to carry out the plan—not the counselor.

Crisis counseling also focuses on an immediate threat or event, but leaves control of the conversation and the decisions in the hands of the counselee as the counselor skillfully offers guidance.

Short-term Counseling

Short-term counseling focuses on short-term problems and events: premarital counseling, career counseling, grief counseling, conflict resolution. The focus is on the present crisis or situation. Friends, pastors, and professional counselors all become involved in short-term counseling. In short-term counseling, the pressure is not there to make an immediate decision or to take immediate action.

Long-term Counseling

Long-term counseling deals with problems that take a longer time to resolve, such as, alcohol and drug addictions, mental and emotional problems, sexual addictions, phobias. Some marital and relational problems require long-term counseling. Again, the pressure for immediate action and response is not as intense as in the cases of crisis intervention and crisis counseling. Thus, the person needing long-term counseling can call and make an appointment with a professional counselor.

Long-term counseling sessions take place in a counselor's office or at a rehabilitation center, mental health clinic, or family and marriage counseling center. There, the client meets with a psychologist or psychiatrist, who performs an in-depth analysis of the client's history, examining his or her childhood, marital problems, interpersonal relationships, basic attitudes, thought patterns, personality conflicts, addictive behavior, compulsions, mental depression. A psychiatrist is also a physician and can prescribe medication when needed.

How Can I Help? will equip you with skills for crisis intervention, crisis counseling, and short-term counseling. You will also gain insight into making a referral when it becomes apparent an individual needs long-term or professional counseling.

As a lay counselor, you must be aware of your limitations and be prepared to call on others for their expertise when you are unable to help. You should feel free to call a pastor or professional counselor to help someone in crisis, just as you would call a medical doctor to repair a broken bone or a lawyer to represent you in court. Most of the time, however, a person in crisis simply needs the loving, comforting arms of a friend.

Take a moment before reading further to do the exercise on page 13. Consider how you would respond to each of these people if he or she turned to you and made the statement indicated. Write your response in the space provided.

The material in this course teaches counseling responses and evangelistic tools that will help you in situations similar to these, as well as in others. You will learn five phases of a counseling model to help you guide people through the three stages of crisis. The counseling model that is presented is an integrated Christian counseling model, which you will look at in the next chapter. This model will help you to integrate your personal counseling skills with your Christian faith. You will see how you can lead a person to Jesus in a gentle, nonthreatening way. And you will study the way Jesus counseled and helped people, and how, as His modern-day disciple, His Holy Spirit will counsel through you.

This course teaches itself, so you can study it with a group or on your own. In the text you will find role plays, exercises, and homework to complete and hand in to your group leader. If you are studying this on your own, do the homework for your own review. And if you can, find a friend or family member to do the role plays with you so you can practice the counseling techniques.

NOTE: If you are studying this with a group, please complete the registration and the Personal Beliefs Survey at the end of this chapter and hand in to your small group leader with the following exercise.

I commend you for your interest in helping others. This course has been tremendously effective in equipping Christians all over the world. I know that God will use it to develop your counseling and evangelism skills. God wants to use you to comfort and counsel the hurting people around you.

EXERCISE

Name _____

Date _____

Group Leader _____

Write your responses to the following remarks.

Hand this in to your small group leader at the end of the class.

1. **Elderly Lady:** "I've been so lonesome since my husband died."

   _____
   _____
   _____
   _____
   _____

2. **College Student:** "I can't seem to cope anymore."

   _____
   _____
   _____
   _____
   _____

3. **Woman:** "My husband hit me again. He's been drinking."

   _____
   _____
   _____
   _____
   _____

4. **Young Girl:** "What do you do when nobody cares?"

   _____
   _____
   _____
   _____

5. **Woman:** "My husband moved out. He said he doesn't love me anymore."

_____

_____

_____

_____

_____

6. **Close Friend:** "I saw the doctor today. I have cancer. They are going to operate Wednesday and (pause) I want you to have my stamp collection."

_____

_____

_____

_____

_____

7. **Sister:** "I found drugs in my son's room. I don't know what to do. I'm afraid that if I say anything, he'll run away."

_____

_____

_____

_____

_____

_____

8. **Spouse:** "Honey, sit down. Our daughter is pregnant and she is going to have an abortion."

_____

_____

_____

_____

_____

_____

Registration

Please take a moment to register.

My name is _____ Date _____

I attend _____ Church

My mailing address is _____

_____ Zip _____

My telephone number is _____ (day) _____ (night)

I am: ___ Single ___ Married ___ Separated ___ Divorced
___ Widowed

My Birthday is ___/___/___/   My age is _____

I have _____ Child(ren) Ages _____

My spouse's name is _____

My occupation is _____

My interests include:

___ Assisting in Office   ___ Counseling
___ Teaching   ___ Support Group
___ Visitation   ___ Serving on Committee
___ Serving wherever needed

The time I am most available to volunteer is _____

Please check one response:
___ I am under the care of a professional counselor.
___ I have been under the care of a professional counselor.
___ I have never been under the care of a professional counselor.

If I died tonight,
___ I know for sure that I would go to heaven.
___ I think that I would go to heaven.
___ I am not sure that I would go to heaven.

If I were in a traffic accident and died, and the time had come for me to stand before God, and He said to me, "Why should I let you into heaven?" I would say:

_____

_____

Personal Beliefs Survey

This is a confidential survey. Do not sign your name.

Indicate your personal belief regarding the following activity or behavior.

	YES	NOT SURE	NO
Sex before marriage is a sin.	—	—	—
Sex outside of marriage is a sin.	—	—	—
Divorce is a sin.	—	—	—
Homosexuality is a sin.	—	—	—
Smoking/Overeating is a sin.	—	—	—
Driving 80 mph is a sin.	—	—	—
Not attending church is a sin.	—	—	—
Not forgiving someone is a sin.	—	—	—
Reading your horoscope is a sin.	—	—	—
Wearing a revealing swimsuit in public is a sin.	—	—	—
Having sexual fantasies about various people is a sin.	—	—	—
Looking at a *Playboy* magazine is a sin.	—	—	—
Watching an X-rated movie is a sin.	—	—	—
Masturbation is a sin.	—	—	—
Listening to dirty jokes is a sin.	—	—	—
Using profanity is a sin.	—	—	—

Gossip is a sin. — — —

Holding anger in your heart is a sin. — — —

Self-pity is a sin. — — —

Not receiving Jesus Christ as your
personal Savior is a sin. — — —

Getting drunk is a sin. — — —

Not doing your best is a sin. — — —

Abortion for personal convenience is
a sin. — — —

Worry is a sin. — — —

Not paying your bills is a sin. — — —

Driving while intoxicated is a sin. — — —

HOMEWORK
Chapter 1

Name _____

Date _____

Group Leader _____

Hand in to small group leader in class two.

Match the word with the definition:

___ 1. Developmental crisis   A. A series of events
___ 2. Accidental crisis   B. An imagined threat
___ 3. Actual crisis   C. A sudden occurrence
___ 4. Potential crisis   D. An anticipated event
___ 5. Compound crisis   E. A real event
___ 6. Chronic crisis   F. A continuous state of crisis

7. The two symbols in the Chinese word for "crisis" stand for: _____ and _____.

8. The three stages of a crisis are: _____, _____, and _____.

9. Crisis involves a significant _____.

10. In crisis _____ the person in crisis remains in control.

11. In crisis _____ the counselor takes control.

12. A psychiatrist is also a _____ and can _____ _____.

13. Memory Verse: Write out Romans 8:28.

_____

_____

_____

14. Memory Verse: Write out Galatians 5:22.

_____

_____

_____

(1) _____ (2) _____ (3) _____
(4) _____ (5) _____ (6) _____
(7) _____ (8) _____ (9) _____

CLOSING DEVOTION
The Call to Ministry

In the King James Version of John 14:16, Jesus said, "I will pray the Father, and he shall give you another Comforter." The same Scripture verse in the New International Version reports Jesus saying, "I will ask the Father, and he will give you another Counselor." God sends His Holy Spirit to minister through us. He is the Comforter. He is the Counselor. He will minister through us as we yield to Him.

The CALL to ministry is to ALL CHRISTIANS.

The GOAL of ministry is to LEAD OTHERS TO CHRIST.

The POWER for ministry is HIS HOLY SPIRIT.

The GUIDE for ministry is HIS HOLY BIBLE.

The PREPARATION for ministry is PRAYER.

The ACTION for ministry is OBEDIENCE.

The MOTIVE for ministry is LOVE.

The REWARD for ministry is JOY.

The RESULT of ministry is PEACE.

The BEGINNING of ministry is PATIENCE.

The EXPRESSION of ministry is KINDNESS.

The CHARACTER of ministry is GOODNESS.

The COMMITMENT of ministry is FAITHFULNESS.

The APPROACH of ministry is GENTLENESS.

The VICTORY of ministry is SELF CONTROL.

The MODEL for ministry is JESUS!

Closing Prayer

Chapter 2

Integrated Counseling Model

Counseling can be separated into two broad areas: secular and Christian, as shown in the chart that follows. *Secular* is defined as "temporal rather than spiritual; worldly; not religious" *(Webster's II New Revised Dictionary)*. In secular counseling, a person attempts to help man with his problems without involving God. Into this category fall the non-Christian and Christian secular counselor.

SECULAR COUNSELING		CHRISTIAN COUNSELING	
NON-CHRISTIAN	CHRISTIAN	INTEGRATED	EVANGELISTIC

Many *non-Christian secular psychologists and psychiatrists* believe religion imposes guilt and causes problems. At times, their underlying principles, theories, and counsel contradict the

Word of God. Many of these counselors, for example, condone homosexuality and premarital sex as appropriate behavior. The *Christian secular counselor* on the other hand offers counsel, hopefully, that is consistent with the Word of God and is himself a Christian. But in every other respect he operates as the non-Christian secular counselor operates. He does not confront sinful behavior or lead a person into a relationship with Jesus Christ or His Holy Spirit.

Because the principles taught in secular counseling courses and practiced by secular psychologists, psychiatrists, and counselors often contradict the teachings of the Bible, many Christians have taken the position that all psychology or secular counseling is bad. Those who take this position usually fall into the category of the evangelistic Christian counselor.

The *evangelistic Christian counselor* believes that man is lost in sin and must be saved before he can deal effectively with personal problems. He believes that for a total and complete healing the spiritual life of a person must be addressed. The powerful unconditional, or agape, love of God must be brought into the counseling process. Only Jesus can take away our sins. Only the Holy Spirit can give us true victory and the power to live a new and transformed life. Thus, introducing a person to Jesus and to the Holy Spirit and interceding in prayer for God to work in the person's life play an integral part of the evangelistic Christian counselor's help.

Evangelistic Christian counselors are usually zealous, deeply committed Christians. However, people often perceive them as pushing their faith onto others or "overspiritualizing," approaching every problem from only a spiritual perspective. In the end, the evangelistic Christian counselors often drive away the very people they are trying to help. The problem is not with what they believe, however; it is with when and how they present the truth.

The model I use in this course is an *integrated Christian counseling* model. We depend upon Scripture, Christ's example, the Holy Spirit, and biblically sound counseling principles for the counseling techniques and principles we use and the advice we offer. *We trust in the Holy Bible as our final authority.* We use it to discern truth from falsehood.

Many principles of secular and humanistic psychology are riddled with error and contradiction of God's Word. But secular counselors have also made significant discoveries in the areas of psychological testing, child development, interpersonal relationships, personal communication, attitude changes, the nature of personality, and the influence of drugs. These discoveries are helpful and they do not contradict the Word of God.

Scripture says that all truth comes from God. He is the Way, the Truth, and the Life. Thus, we should consider using these teachings, even though they have been discovered by a secular psychologist or counselor. A Christian doctor would use a medicine or medical technique discovered by a non-Christian. Similarly, we as Christian counselors can use all of the skills and techniques available to us that are consistent with the Word of God.

What follows is an integrated Christian counseling model—that is, it combines biblically sound counseling principles and techniques with the Gospel of Jesus Christ and other Scriptural promises. The outline is a pattern for life, as well as a map for the course. It will guide you as you help friends in crisis.

THE INTEGRATED COUNSELING MODEL

The integrated counseling model is comprised of five phases. As you can see in the following chart, it is divided into two parts, personal and spiritual. We will focus on personal counseling in Part One of this course and on spiritual counseling in Part Two. A picture word outlines what is accomplished in each phase. Study the model. Memorize the picture words. This counseling model will change your life!

PERSONAL		SPIRITUAL		
PERSON	PROBLEM	PERSONAL RELATIONSHIP	PERSONAL BEHAVIOR	PERSONAL MINISTRY
ARMS	HELP	LOVE	CARE	CHRIST

ARMS

When people are hurting and in crisis, they first need for us to reach out to them with our ARMS. Most of the people who turn to us for help have been rejected. So they need us to be nonjudgmental and accepting. We need to listen to what they have to say. The picture word is ARMS:

A —*Accept* the person.
R —*Reflect* what the person is saying and feeling.
M —*Motivate* the person to talk.
S —*Support* the person.

In chapter 3, you will learn about attitudes that help and attitudes that hurt in the counseling process. You will also learn some valuable listening skills and counseling responses that will help you reflect what a person is saying and motivate him to talk.

HELP

In the second phase of the counseling model, we begin to HELP the individual focus on the problem and evaluate his options and alternatives. Our picture word is HELP:

H —*Help* identify and prioritize problems.
E —*Evaluate* options and alternatives.
L —*Lend* ideas for consideration.
P —*Help* develop a plan.

Chapter 5 will present interactive responses, including open-ended questions you can use in helping a person consider various options and alternatives. You will learn how to lend ideas and help a person develop specific goals and plans without telling the person what to do.

Most secular counselors stop after establishing a relationship with the person and offering help with the problem. Having focused on the person and helped with the problem, their mission is complete. As Christian counselors, however, we have the opportunity to lead the conversation into the spiritual area at this point. We are concerned about a person's relationship with God and want to offer His LOVE. The last three phases of the integrated counseling model involve spiritual counseling.

LOVE

In the third phase, we discover if the person has a personal relationship with Jesus Christ and offer God's LOVE—that is, we

L —*Lead* the conversation into the spiritual area.
O—*Offer* God's love and plan of salvation through Jesus Christ.
V — *Verify* the Holy Spirit's presence and power, and
E —*Encourage* the person to join the fellowship of a local church.

In chapter 8, you will learn the exciting Home Run Presentation of the Gospel, which will help you introduce family and friends to Jesus Christ in a natural, nonthreatening way.

After a person has come to Jesus Christ, he has the indwelling presence of the Holy Spirit. Now, he has the power within himself to change his behavior, so we move into the fourth phase.

CARE

In this phase, we turn our attention to the person's behavior with CARE. That is, we

C—*Confront* sinful behavior, knowing that the Holy Spirit will convict the person of his sin. Lead him to confess his sin and change his behavior. In the process of doing this you must help the person to become

A—*Aware* of what the Bible says regarding specific behavior, leading the person to

R—*Repent* of his sinful behavior, and

E—*Encourage* him to walk in obedience to God's Word in fellowship with the Holy Spirit.

Chapter 12 will provide insights to help you know how and when to confront sinful, destructive behavior. You will also learn how to help a person change his thoughts and desires, as well as his behavior.

Once a person has come to Jesus Christ and allowed the Holy Spirit to transform his behavior, God calls that person to personal ministry.

CHRIST

As we guide a person into an intimate relationship with Jesus Christ and prepare him for personal ministry, we will be fulfilling the Great Commission, to "Go therefore and make disciples" (Matt. 28:19). In this final counseling phase, CHRIST is the word picture:

C—*Commitment!* God calls us to make a deep commitment. "Take up your cross," Jesus said. There is a cost in being a disciple.

H—His *Holy Spirit* will go with us, however. He must truly be in control of our lives. We must

R—*Read* and study God's Word,

I—*Involve* Jesus in all of our decisions; intercede for others, and go forth

S—*Serving* others,

T—*Teaching* and sharing with them all that God has revealed to us.

Christ alive in us is the ultimate goal of this integrated Christian counseling model. Our mission is to help people establish a personal relationship with Jesus Christ as Savior and Lord and to develop the skills of discipleship through the church and its various ministries, including Christian colleges and parachurch ministries. This does not mean that every counseling interview or crisis call should include a presentation of the Gospel. It does mean that after we have developed a relationship with someone and addressed his crisis situation, it is appropriate to proceed with a presentation of the Gospel and other spiritual counseling.

If you are a member of a group using this book, proceed with the following exercise. Otherwise, go on to the devotion.

EXERCISE
How Do You Do?

Group Leader's Name _____

Date _____ Telephone number _____

Divide the class into small groups of 8 to 10 people. Have each group choose a leader. Write your leader's name and telephone number in the space provided.

Find someone you do not know in your small group and spend about ten minutes getting to know each other. Find out three interesting things about each other and be prepared to introduce that person to the group. Be careful that one person doesn't do all the talking. Take notes to help you remember what you learn about your partner.

Name _____

1. _____

_____

2. _____
   _____
   _____
   _____
   _____

3. _____
   _____
   _____
   _____
   _____

As you listen to the other members of your group being introduced, you may want to take notes in the space provided. You can review your notes during the week to help you remember the people in your group. Next week you'll be able to call them by name.

Other People in the Group	Things of Interest

Other People in the Group

_____

_____

_____

_____

_____

_____

_____

_____

_____

_____

_____

_____

_____

_____

_____

_____

_____

_____

_____

_____

_____

_____

_____

_____

_____

_____

_____

_____

_____

_____

Things of Interest

_____

_____

_____

_____

_____

_____

_____

_____

_____

_____

_____

_____

_____

_____

_____

_____

_____

_____

_____

_____

_____

_____

_____

_____

_____

_____

_____

_____

_____

_____

CLOSING DEVOTION
Acceptance
Jesus and the Woman
Caught in Adultery
John 8:2–11

Now early in the morning He came again into the temple, and all the people came to Him; and He sat down and taught them. Then the scribes and Pharisees brought to Him a woman caught in adultery. And when they had set her in the midst, they said to Him, "Teacher, this woman was caught in adultery, in the very act. Now Moses, in the law, commanded us that such should be stoned. But what do You say?" This they said, testing Him, that they might have something of which to accuse Him.

The scribes and Pharisees thought they had trapped Jesus. Mosaic Law said that a person who committed adultery was to be put to death. Roman Law prohibited the Jews from invoking the death penalty. Whatever Jesus said, they figured they had trapped Him.

But Jesus stooped down and wrote on the ground with His finger, as though He did not hear. So when they continued asking Him, He raised Himself up and said to them, "He who is without sin among you, let him throw a stone at her first." And again He stooped down and wrote on the ground.

Then those who heard it, being convicted by their conscience, went out one by one, beginning with the oldest even to the last. And Jesus was left alone, and the woman standing in the midst.

When Jesus had raised Himself up and saw no one

but the woman, He said to her, "Woman, where are those accusers of yours? Has no one condemned you?" She said, "No one, Lord." And Jesus said to her, "Neither do I condemn you; go and sin no more" (John 8:2–11).

We must be able to separate the sinner from his behavior the way Jesus did. As we accept the person, we will be able to lead him to the Lord who will enable him to receive forgiveness and sin no more.

Closing Prayer

Chapter 3

Reach Out with ARMS: Part I

When I was a teenager, my best friend, Hank, would come to our house whenever he was upset. We would go for a long ride in his car. Hank would drive and talk, and I would sit and listen.

Hank was in control. He was the driver, and I was the passenger. That's the way it needs to be when people turn to us for help. They need to be in control. Often, they have lost control of significant areas of their lives. Hurting and confused, they need acceptance and love. And they need to be in control of the conversation!

If I had jumped in and started asking Hank a lot of questions, or begun giving a lot of advice, it would have been like my jerking the steering wheel out of his hands. What he needed was for me to care, for me to be with him, for me to listen.

FOCUS ON THE PERSON

When someone asks for help, the natural tendency is to focus on the problem and begin asking questions. Unfortunately, this makes the person feel like an object and as though no one cares.

If a little girl falls and scratches her leg, what does she need from her mother? Does she need for her mother to scold her or blame her? "You should have been more careful. I told you not to . . ." Does she even want her mother to "fix" her leg right away?

No. Instead, she needs her mother's arms around her. She wants her mother to accept her, to love her, to listen to her, and to care about her. The mother needs to identify with her, and reflect back what she is saying and feeling. She needs to motivate her daughter to talk in order to discover what has happened. The mother is there to support and comfort her child. Then, after her child feels loved and comforted, the mother can focus on the problem of her scraped leg.

As long as the daughter's scrape is not a medical emergency, demanding immediate treatment, she needs her mother to focus the attention on her and embrace her with ARMS. We defined the acrostic ARMS in the last chapter as Accept, Reflect, Motivate, Support.

Attitudes in counseling are important—not only the attitudes of the counselor but the attitudes of the counselee. Consider Andy and George.

THE ATTITUDE OF THE COUNSELEE

Andy and George were both district managers in a welding supply company that was acquired by a large corporation. In time the large corporation made several management changes, and both Andy and George lost their jobs.

Andy was depressed and defeated. Twenty years in the welding supply business. Now, he would have to start all over.

George was optimistic and hopeful. Twenty years in the welding supply business! Now, he had enough experience and contacts to start a business of his own.

Both men faced the same situation with similar experience,

skills, and opportunities. One looked at the situation with a negative attitude, and took months even to begin looking for another job. The other, however, had a positive attitude, so he adjusted more quickly. Within a few months George had his new business up and going.

A person's attitude, positive or negative, can determine how well he or she moves through the stages of crisis. Some people have a positive mental attitude. They do not deny problems or pain; rather, they meet them head-on. They grieve and they hurt, but they make choices that help them bring about positive changes. A person's experience with crisis; his maturity and willingness to assume responsibility; his physical and financial condition; and his relationship with Jesus Christ, as well as the presence of friends, a pastor, or a counselor or support group, affect how long and how deeply a person experiences a crisis and the completeness with which he recovers. Self-talk can also affect how a person deals with crisis.

A person can say positive, hopeful things to himself, or he can fill his mind with negative thoughts and ideas. This self-talk shapes his attitudes and perceptions. If Andy, the district manager from the welding business, tells himself he will never get a job now that he has been laid off—he is too old—he will be demotivated and won't look for a job. If Andy tells himself that he, like George, has all the potential in the world, he will be more likely to find work.

The Word of God says, "as he thinks in his heart, so is he" (Prov. 23:7). If we think positively, and trust in God, we will be able to have the faith to get us through crisis. Instead of a positive attitude of faith, though, some people choose to live with one or more negative attitudes that keep them in a rut and prevent them from working through their problems.

Fear

Some people live with a negative attitude of fear. They constantly worry and fret. They are unsure and fearful about life.

Everyone lives at some point between faith and fear, between a positive mental attitude and a negative one. Clearly, the Word of God tells us to think positive thoughts and to have faith whereas it speaks of worry, fear, and anxiety as sins. To hold on to these emotions means that we are not trusting God. "I sought the LORD, and He heard me, / And delivered me from all my fears" (Ps. 34:4). "For God has not given us a spirit of fear, but of power and of love and of a sound mind" (2 Tim. 1:7).

Self-pity

Another negative attitude that can control people in crisis and keep them from moving toward recovery is self-pity. Remember Diana, from chapter 1? When her husband, Jerry, left, she fell into the pit of self-pity. For a time the sympathy she received from her children and her friends replaced the "love" she had lost. Ultimately, the self-pity immobilized her and sent her into deep depression.

As long as people hold on to self-pity, they will be depressed. An emotionally healthy person does not seek ways to invoke sympathy from family and friends. Manipulated sympathy is a poor substitute for love and true concern and will burn out friends fast. Eventually, the depressed person must confess his self-pity as a sin and "know that all things work together for good to those who love God, to those who are the called according to His purpose" (Rom. 8:28).

Anger

Being angry about the behavior and actions of a person differs from holding on to anger and bitterness toward a person. A healthy, or positive, person will acknowledge the pain another person has caused, be angry about it, and move on. An unhealthy person will hold on to resentment and unforgiveness.

The person in crisis may be the victim of another person's

actions or sinful behavior. But he still must forgive this person. God tells us to "love [our] enemies" (Matt. 5:44).

If a person in crisis is holding on to anger against a person, he must confess that as a sin and forgive the person who has hurt him.

Blaming God

Many times people in crisis will blame God for allowing tragic circumstances to occur. Diana wanted to blame God for Jerry's leaving. But Christian friends helped her see that God gives man freedom to choose, and some people choose sin. Sin offers pleasure. And it sometimes seems the sinner gets away free while the victim receives the pain. Although this can leave the "victim" feeling angry at God, the victim must realize that God's will is not always done. God did not want Jerry to become involved with another woman and divorce Diana. But God did love Diana through the pain of the event, and He would work all things together for her good, because she loved Him (see Rom. 8:28).

Besides negative attitudes, a person's desire for change can also affect how long it takes to move through a crisis.

DESIRE OF THE COUNSELEE

People must recognize and acknowledge that their problems exist if they are to recover successfully from crisis. They must acknowledge their problems and desire to change. If people do not acknowledge having problems or desire to change, they are not going to look for solutions. Counseling at this point is ineffective.

In marriage counseling, one spouse often refuses to recognize that there is a problem. He or she may be holding on to a behavior, not wanting to change. This makes it difficult to help the couple work on or change their relationship. Jerry and Diana, from chapter 1 for example, were unable to work through their problems for this reason.

Counseling didn't help Jerry and Diana because Jerry didn't really want to go. "I don't have any problems!" he would bluster. Jerry had a girlfriend, a wife, two grown children, a house, a high paying job, and some good drinking buddies. He did not want to confront or change his behavior.

A positive mental attitude and a determined desire to change are critical for constructive changes to take place. God will not intervene and overpower a person. The person with sinful behavior must repent, turn to Jesus Christ, and desire to change.

The victim must choose to give up his self-pity and anger by repenting in the Name of Jesus Christ and changing his thoughts and mental attitude. If he does so, God will forgive him and he will have taken the first step in overcoming depression. The anger must be replaced with forgiveness, the self-pity with faith. Diana continued in counseling, even after the divorce. Because she was seeking help, the counselor was able to help her.

The Scriptures provide some promises that can help us maintain a positive attitude of faith:

God loves us (see John 3:16).

God has a plan and a purpose for our lives (see Phil. 2:13).

"All things work together for good to those who love God, to those who are the called according to His purpose" (Rom. 8:28).

THE ATTITUDES OF THE COUNSELOR

The attitude of the counselor or helping friend will quickly determine whether the person in crisis will open up and share his problems, trust and confide in him, and receive his counsel and help. People in crisis want friends to warmly accept them, to comfort them, to reach out and care. They need someone who will listen and try to understand what they are feeling and what is happening in their life. They want that person to be genuine and to take the time to truly understand their situation. And finally, they want their counselor to offer ideas, thoughts, and suggestions. But they want to make their own decisions.

People do not want to be probed with a lot of questions or to be given advice before their situation is fully understood. They don't need explanations or judgment or blame.

People in crisis don't need criticism, condemnation, or sermonizing, nor do they want others to try to get their minds off their problems by diverting their attention or by changing the subject.

If you are studying this course with a group of people, take a moment to discuss the following. Appoint one person to read the exercise. Everyone else should close the book and listen. The reader will occasionally pause for your comments. If you are reading this book on your own, pause where indicated and write in the appropriate spaces how you are feeling.

ATTITUDES THAT HELP	
Warm	Genuine
Accepting	Patient
Caring	Empathetic
Listening	Nondirective

ATTITUDES THAT HURT	
Questioning	Judging
Advising	Moralizing
Explaining	Diverting

You are on the way to the drug store. You pull into the parking lot as it begins to rain. You spot two parking places right by the front door. You start to pull in to one of the parking spaces when, out of nowhere, this little red sports car drives in front of you and takes up both parking spaces.

A young man jumps out of the car and runs into the drug store just as the rain really begins to come down hard. He doesn't wave or acknowledge you in any way. He has taken up both spaces and simply disappeared. You, on the other hand, have to park two rows over. You wait for a break in the rain and when you get halfway from your car to the store, it begins to rain again. You reach the front door of the drug store soaking wet.

How do you feel? What do you think you would say to the young man who took up the two parking spaces if you were to see him right now? Has this kind of thing ever happened to you before?

(Pause for comments or fill in the space.)

_____

_____

_____

_____

_____

You are in the drug store and you are going down the aisle with your shopping cart when a young man, a different young man, bumps into your shopping cart. He almost knocks you down. He doesn't apologize or anything. He just pushes past and goes on down the aisle.

How do you feel? What is your attitude toward the young man who just bumped into you?

(Pause for comments or write in your response.)

_____

_____

_____

_____

_____

You finally locate the things you are looking for and check out without anything else happening. The rain has stopped and you quickly get into your car. You turn out onto the main boulevard and about three blocks away, you come to a major intersection where there has been an accident. A school bus filled with Boy Scouts has pulled over to one side of the road. It was involved in the accident. In the middle of the intersection, an Emergency Medical Unit is treating a little old lady. Her small car is being towed off. There is an old pickup truck in the intersection. The police are talking to the driver. He is young and looks pretty rough. He is unshaved and his clothes are dirty.

As you drive past, you notice that one of the policemen, talking to the driver of the truck, is holding a six pack of beer.

> What are your thoughts about drinking and driving?
> What are your feelings toward the young man who was driving the truck?
> What are your feelings for the lady?

(Pause for comments or write your responses.)

_____

_____

_____

_____

_____

You drive past the accident and on to the hospital to visit your Aunt Kate. As you pull into the hospital parking lot—you can't believe it—there are two parking spaces right by the front door!

Just as you are pulling into one of the parking spaces, that young man, that same young man, the one in the little red sports car who left you soaking wet at the drug store, pulls up and parks right next to you!

No mistake. That's him.

You both get out of your cars at the same time.

OK, it's your turn. He looks at you. What do you say to him?

(Pause for comments or write your response.)

_____

_____

_____

_____

_____

He explains to you that he is a Boy Scout Leader with the local Boy Scout Troop. He and the Scoutmaster, the young man who was driving the pickup truck, were returning from a camping trip with the troop when a little old lady, who had been drinking, ran the traffic light and ran into the school bus. Several of the boys were cut by the resulting broken glass, but he and another parent, the man who ran into your shopping cart, were able to get some first aid supplies and bandages at the drug store. He explains that several of the boys are in the Emergency Room now and he is on his way to be with them.

How do you feel?

We've been tricked, huh? This was all in fun, but the points made are valid:

- Appearances can be deceiving.
- Behavior may be caused by factors unknown.

In counseling, we must reserve judgment and maintain an open attitude. James 1:19 says, "Let every man be swift to hear, slow to speak." In the next chapter we will take a look at some counseling responses that will help us to listen and reflect what a person is saying and feeling instead of jump to conclusions.

HOMEWORK
Chapter 3

Name _____

Date _____

Group Leader _____

Hand in to Group Leader in your next class.

True—T   False—F

___ 1. Significant change is normally associated with a personal crisis.

___ 2. Mental attitude, positive or negative, has little effect on the way in which a person conducts himself during a crisis.

___ 3. Romans 8:28 says that "most things work together for good."

___ 4. For a situation to change, a person must recognize that a problem exists, and he must desire to bring about a change.

___ 5. As long as a person holds on to self-pity and unforgiveness, he will be subject to bouts of depression.

___ 6. A positive mental attitude and a determined desire for change are critical for constructive changes to take place.

___ 7. Forgiveness and faith are two important keys to overcoming depression.

8. Identify attitudes that help with a Y for Yes. Identify attitudes that hurt with an N for No.

We should be . . .

___ Accepting	___ Advising	___ Helpful
___ Caring	___ Listening	___ Explaining
___ Diverting	___ Questioning	___ Patient
___ Warm	___ Empathetic	___ Moralizing
___ Judging	___ Genuine	___ Non-directive

9. Memory Verse: Write out Proverbs 23:7, KJV.

_____

_____

_____

_____

_____

10. Memory Verse: Write out John 14:26, KJV.

_____

_____

_____

_____

_____

CLOSING DEVOTION
Jesus and Zacchaeus
Luke 19:1–9

Jesus was walking through Jericho for the last time, on His way to the cross in Jerusalem. In Jericho, there was a man by the name of Zacchaeus who was a very wealthy tax collector. Zacchaeus was a Jew who had "sold out" to the Roman government. He used Roman soldiers to beat people and to extort tax money. Excess taxing made Zacchaeus very rich and very much hated by the people of Jericho. Zacchaeus had no doubt heard many things about Jesus, and he wanted to see Him as He passed though Jericho. Being a short man, Zacchaeus could not see above the crowds that surrounded Jesus. So Zacchaeus ran ahead and climbed up into a sycamore tree to see Jesus, as He walked past.

When Jesus reached the sycamore tree in whose limbs Zacchaeus was hiding, Jesus looked up and said, "Zacchaeus, come down immediately. I must stay at your house today." So, Zacchaeus came down at once and welcomed Jesus into his home.

This was the last time that Jesus would be in Jericho. He could have preached to the whole community. He had the attention of everyone. He could have called a meeting of all the religious and political leaders in town. Instead, Jesus went home with the most hated man in town.

The people saw this and began to mutter, "He has gone to be the guest of a sinner." They didn't understand, and to be honest, it would probably have been misunderstood today as well. It is probably not what most of us would have done.

Most people, if they had the attention of everybody in town, would spend their time talking to the crowd. If they could meet with anybody, wouldn't they pull together the "power group," the leaders of the community? Or, if this was the last time a person would be in Jericho, wouldn't he want to spend the time with the faithful body of believers?

Christians get all caught up talking about ministry. Jesus demonstrated ministry. Christians get excited when an opportunity comes to talk to a large crowd. Jesus spent most of His time ministering to one person at a time. Christians become concerned about problems and develop programs. Jesus concerned Himself with people one at a time.

Because Jesus cared about Zacchaeus, He befriended the most hated man in town. This enabled Zacchaeus to turn away from his sins and call Jesus, Lord!!

Time and time again, we see Jesus separating the sinner from their sinful behavior. He loved and accepted the person, but not their sinful behavior.

Closing Prayer

Chapter 4

Reach Out with ARMS: Part II

Have you ever been listening to someone when your mind wandered? One minute you are right there with your friend. Then suddenly, your mind is a million miles away. Before you know it, you've missed half of what was said and you're trying to catch up with the conversation. It's difficult to do, isn't it?

Listening is hard work. It is an act of love, a gift of yourself and of your time. And it is essential to the overall counseling process. The following seven steps will help you become a more effective listener:

1. **Give up control.** Be willing to listen. Set aside the inner urge to think about what you are going to say when the person stops talking.

2. **Give your undivided attention.** Focus on the other person, listen intently, maintain eye contact without staring, remove distractions, and pay attention to facial expressions. Watery

eyes, glances, tight lips, tone of voice, crossed arms, and other gestures often indicate what the person is feeling.

3. **Suspend judgment; don't try to solve the problem.** Listen impartially and withhold judgment until after you have heard the "whole story." Resist jumping in and trying to solve the problem. The effective counselor/friend helps the person to reason through his situation and reach sound decisions, having considered his various options and their consequences.

4. **Listen for feelings.** Listen carefully for the person's feelings and respond empathetically. Ask yourself, "How would I feel if I were in this situation?"

5. **Listen for the dominant concern.** Sometimes the person will discuss several different problems and precipitating events. Listen for the dominant recurring subject. This will help you identify the area of greatest concern. Recognize that the presenting problem may not be the main problem. As the person learns to trust you, he will reveal additional areas of concern.

6. **Provide feedback.** Reflect brief comments, showing what you hear the other person saying and feeling. Reflections help the person to know he is being heard and understood.

7. **Summarize.** Give a brief summary of what your friend has said to make sure you've received an accurate message. This can also help him see his situation more clearly and gain perspective.

These steps form the basis for the active listening responses you will use to draw out the content of what a person is saying and identify his feelings. You will use them as you help someone evaluate his situation and establish goals and objectives and plans.

ACTIVE LISTENING RESPONSES

Active listening motivates the person to talk. It allows you to conduct a one-way conversation, in which the person in crisis does most of the talking. As you apply the techniques of the first phase of the counseling model, your role is simply to listen and reflect what the person is saying and feeling.

The responses we will discuss in the next two chapters can be used at any time in the counseling process. Although you remain nondirective while you are in phase one, you may want to take notes as you listen. These will come in handy in phase two, when you are problem-solving and evaluating a person's needs and resources.

Conversational Response

Conversational responses come naturally to us. We use them in everyday dialogue. While someone is talking to us, we reply, "Uh huh," "I see," "Oh," "Hmm." These are conversational responses. They let the other person know that we are paying attention. But they do not get in the way or interrupt. Instead, conversational responses allow the other person to continue talking. Write a conversational response to each of the following statements:

Example:

"If I can't get the house refinanced, I'll lose it!"

"Oh no!"

"I think I'll get the job at Sears."

_____

_____

_____

"This is the third time the car has broken down."

_____

_____

_____

_____

"I just can't seem to make this relationship work."

_____

_____

_____

Mirror Response

A mirror response reflects everything that is placed in front of it. You give a mirror response by repeating back to the person talking whatever he or she just said. If a person says, "One, two, three," you would say, "One, two, three." Consider this example:

Friend: I lost my job and the rent's due.

Counselor: You lost your job and the rent's due.

Write a mirror response to the following statements.

"Nobody cares about me."

_____

_____

_____

"The washing machine is broken again."

_____

_____

_____

"I can't seem to cope anymore."

_____

_____

_____

Content Response

Whereas the mirror response reflects almost the same words the person has just said, the content response reflects only part of what has been said. You can begin to sound like an echo if you use the mirror response too much in one conversation. This can become irritating after a while. So, with a content response, you turn the mirror slightly and reflect only a part of what the person is saying. If a person says, "One, two, three," the content response might be, "Oh, two." An example of this might be the following:

Friend: He ran the stop sign and I hit him.

Counselor: You hit him!

Write a content response to the following statements.

"I've been so lonesome since my husband died."

_____

_____

_____

"My husband hit me again. He's been drinking."

_____

_____

_____

"My husband just moved out. He said he doesn't love me anymore."

_____

_____

_____

The second statement is a trick question. If there is physical violence, the situation calls for crisis intervention, not a reflective response. You want to take control and ask if she is hurt, if she needs medical attention, and if she needs you to call the police.

Always focus your response on the most critical part of the statement. In the third statement, for example, reflect "He said he doesn't love you anymore," rather than "he moved out." Your response usually determines the direction of the conversation. In this instance it is more important to focus on the relationship than on the location of the husband.

Feeling Response

People in crisis often react emotionally and make poor decisions. If you can help the hurting person to express his emotions verbally, and thus release his tension, you may prevent him from reacting to his emotions in some harmful way. The feeling response is helpful for doing this.

A feeling response reflects the emotion the person has expressed or implied or can motivate a person to talk about how he feels. The following are feeling responses:

Friend: He just called and said "You're fired."

Counselor: You're really angry.

Or:

"How did that make you feel?"

"Sounds like you are really mad."

"Tell me how you feel right now."

Write a feeling response to each of the following statements.

"I want to quit. I can't do anything right!"

_____

_____

_____

"What do you do when nobody cares?"

_____

_____

_____

"I saw the doctor today. I have cancer, and they are going to operate Wednesday."

_____

_____

_____

"I found drugs in my son's room. I don't know what to do."

_____

_____

_____

Now consider how these responses are used in the following conversation between a forty-year-old woman and a crisis center counselor. If you are in a group, you may want to have two people act this out for the class. Identify what kind of response the counselor is using by checking the appropriate box. After the scene has been acted out, you may want to discuss the responses in your group.

She: I need help. I don't know what to do.

Counselor: You need help?

 ☐ Conversational

 ☐ Mirror

 ☐ Content

 ☐ Feeling

She: I can't control it anymore.

Counselor: (pause) You can't control it anymore.

 ☐ Conversational

 ☐ Mirror

☐ Content

☐ Feeling

She: No, I can't. I started smoking pot three years ago. Then recently, I started smoking crack, and I . . . I . . . (crying) can't control it anymore.

Counselor: (pause) I see.

☐ Conversational

☐ Mirror

☐ Content

☐ Feeling

She: I sold my car. I mortgaged my trailer. I spent all the money on drugs. I've stolen things. I've slept with men. I've done terrible things. (crying) I just can't live like this, but I can't quit. (pause) Driving over here, I passed two drug dealers. You don't know how hard it was not to stop. (pause) They will sell to me on credit. I can't buy groceries, but I can get drugs.

Counselor: (pause) I see.

☐ Conversational

☐ Mirror

☐ Content

☐ Feeling

She: Last night, I threw away my pipe and then at 3 o'clock this morning I was going through the garbage dumpster looking for it—inside the garbage dumpster! (pause) I have got to stop living like this. (pause) I get depressed and I start thinking about drugs. I'll do anything to get the money. Then, I'll lock myself in the bathroom and smoke until I'm sick. I feel horrible when I come down. I'm so scared.

Counselor: (pause) You're scared and you want to stop.

☐ Conversational

☐ Mirror

☐ Content

☐ Feeling

She: Yes, I do!! Can you help me?

In chapter 5 you will learn responses you can use to help this woman and people like her establish goals and objectives.

The counseling responses and attitudes we've discussed in this chapter and the previous one give you the tools to motivate and support someone in crisis.

HOMEWORK
Chapter 4

Name _____

Date _____

Group Leader _____

Write out all four counseling responses to each statement.

Example:

"He said he doesn't love me and just walked out."

A. **Mirror Response**

"He said he doesn't love you and just walked out?"

B. **Conversational Response**

"Oh, no."

C. **Content Response**

"He said he doesn't love you."

D. **Feeling Response**

"I know you're hurting."

1. "Sometimes she really seems to like me, but then she goes off with this other group."

   A. **Mirror Response**

   _____

   _____

   _____

   B. **Conversational Response**

   _____

   _____

   _____

C. Content Response

_____

_____

_____

D. Feeling Response

_____

_____

_____

2. "I'm not sure how I feel anymore. I'm just mad!"

A. Mirror Response

_____

_____

_____

B. Conversational Response

_____

_____

_____

C. Content Response

_____

_____

_____

D. Feeling Response

_____

_____

_____

3. "She should be home by now. She gets off at 5 o'clock."

A. Mirror Response

_____

_____

_____

B. Conversational Response

_____

_____

C. **Content Response**

_____

_____

_____

D. **Feeling Response**

_____

_____

_____

4. "I know he is involved with another woman."
   A. **Mirror Response**

_____

_____

_____

   B. **Conversational Response**

_____

_____

_____

   C. **Content Response**

_____

_____

_____

   D. **Feeling Response**

_____

_____

_____

5. "I'm through with my homework!"
   A. **Mirror Response**

_____

_____

_____

B. **Conversational Response**

_____

_____

_____

C. **Content Response**

_____

_____

_____

D. **Feeling Response**

_____

_____

_____

Give your completed work to your group leader, or keep it to discuss at your next meeting.

CLOSING DEVOTION
Model for Ministry

Jesus Christ, the "Wonderful Counselor" (Isa. 9:6), is our model for ministry. Jesus used a variety of counseling approaches and techniques, depending on the situation, the personality of the people involved, and the intent of the person with whom He was speaking. With Nicodemus, Jesus used an intellectual approach (John 3); with the woman caught in adultery, He was gentle and nonjudgmental (John 8); with the Pharisees who tried to trap Him and confuse the people, He was assertive and confronting (Matt. 22:18–21).

At times, Jesus listened to people and didn't say much, being rather passive and nondirective, reflecting questions back to the person who had asked them, inserting a thought or question here and there (Luke 24:13–35). At times, Jesus demonstrated a love and acceptance of people while demanding repentance from sin and obedience to God's Word.

The same Holy Spirit who taught Jesus and guided Him in His ministry is alive in you. As you yield to Him, He will minister, comfort, and counsel through you.

Closing Prayer

Chapter 5

HELP
Solve the
Problem:
Part I

In the Garden of Eden, Adam and Eve hid from God, not wanting to confront their problem. Today, people are still trying to hide from their problems. They often deny that anything is wrong. And if they do acknowledge their problems, they refuse to deal with them or they blame someone else for them, as did Adam and Eve. People often ignore their problems and hope they will simply go away.

Sometimes people begin to address their problems, but upon meeting with some emotional pain or resistance, they give up and go on. In other instances, problems appear so overwhelming that they turn away from them. People may also fear the consequences of confronting a problem; for example, a wife may not confront her husband's infidelity for fear he will seek a divorce.

Avoiding problems and hoping they will solve themselves or get better is not an effective way to deal with them. Problems do not just go away. Ultimately, they must be addressed.

Using the problem-solving techniques found in phase two of the counseling model, HELP, we encourage people in crisis to overcome denial and accept personal responsibility—major tasks within many counseling situations.

HEREIN LIES THE PROBLEM

We have focused on the person in phase one of the counseling model. We have listened, taken notes, and clarified any confusion.

Now, the person in crisis feels that we care about him. He feels accepted and understood, so we can begin to focus on the problem. We become more interactive in phase two, asking questions that lead a person to evaluate his or her situation, set goals, and make plans to solve the problem. The techniques involved are found in the picture word HELP:

H—*Help* the person identify problems and set priorities.
E—*Evaluate* problem-solving resources, options, and alternatives.
L—*Lend* ideas and possible solutions for consideration.
P—*Plan* immediate steps and direction.

People naturally want to focus on past events and the current situation when they come for help. We need to give ample time to this part of the counseling process so we can gain a thorough understanding of the problem. But people can get stuck in this stage of analyzing the past, attempting to justify their behavior. Productive counseling goes beyond that.

Productive counseling moves a person toward establishing goals and objectives and making plans. It helps the person focus on solutions and positive steps to overcoming specific problems.

Let's take a look at what goals, objectives, and plans are. Then, we will discuss how you can help someone establish them.

GOALS AND PLANS

Goals tell us what we want to achieve. *Objectives* are measurable and tell us how much and by when. *Plans* outline the steps to be taken in obtaining the objective. A person who has been fired from a job may establish the following goal, objective, and plans for finding a new job:

Goal: To obtain an interesting, well-paying job.

Objective: To have at least one job interview each week with a qualified prospective employer.

Plan:
1. Make a list of the type of job/activities I desire to be doing.
2. Make a list of companies that engage in that type of job/activity.
3. Obtain the name of the person who hires, etc.

Establishing goals is especially helpful in marriage counseling with couples who spend their time complaining about each other. It turns their attention to the future and to positive behavior and activity. It changes the focus from blaming the other person for past behavior. The following shows the direction one couple was able to set for themselves:

Goal: To establish harmony in our marital relationship.

Objective: To immediately discontinue all verbal abuse and establish a workable plan for resolving conflicts and making mutually satisfactory decisions.

Plan:
1. Agree not to engage in abusive verbal arguments in the future.

2. When tension begins to rise, agree to discontinue conversation on subject of confrontation for twenty-four hours.
3. Pray together about . . .

Encourage your friend to write down his goals, objectives, and plans. The struggle to find the words to express his goals, describe reasonable objectives, and outline the exact steps to follow will give him tangible results from the counseling session. Writing plans also places the responsibility on the person to proceed in an agreed-upon, prescribed manner and provides a source of accountability for future counseling sessions. You can review, amend, and, if necessary, change the objectives and plans later in future interviews.

Setting goals gives the person talking to you a sense of direction and identifies what he wants to achieve. Establishing objectives defines his goals in reasonable terms—how much and by when. The plan spells it out, 1-2-3: These are the things he must do to achieve the objective.

CHECK FOR THE VITAL SIGNS

Before you can help a person in crisis make plans, you must have some basic information about him. When you go to the doctor, he checks your vital signs to ascertain your condition. The doctor listens to your heartbeat. He takes your temperature, checks your blood pressure, and listens to what you have to say. Likewise, when someone seeks your counsel, you need to assess certain vital areas in order to apply the techniques of HELP.

The following ten areas will help you determine if you have the information you need for problem-solving. You probably have gotten some of this information during phase one. Later in the chapter, we will discuss counseling responses you can use to uncover the answers you do not have about certain vital areas.

1. Physical Condition

What is the physical condition of the person?

Has he been injured?

Does he need medical attention?

Is there a need for intervention?

Does the counselor need to call for the emergency medical service or police?

What are the person's physical needs?

Does he need food, shelter, transportation, etc.?

2. Precipitating Event

In all probability, the person has been living with the problem for some time. What motivated the person to reach out for help now? Was there an argument? Did he hit her?

Understanding the precipitating event can help you better understand the person's immediate thoughts, feelings, and problems.

3. Presenting Problem

Is the problem that is being presented the real problem or simply a symptom of a deeper problem? Many times, the person in crisis will not reveal the real problem right away. You may have to deal with other issues and build a trusting relationship with a person before he will open up and reveal the real problem.

One of the unique advantages of telephone counseling is that the person calling is anonymous. Thus, he or she tends to open up more quickly than he would face-to-face. This is especially true if the face-to-face counselor is his pastor or someone he knows. Even in telephone counseling, however, the counselor must often deal with a presenting problem before getting to the real issue.

4. Personal Perception

What is the person's perception of the situation?

Is he confused? Is his conversation logical?

Is he in touch with reality, dealing with his crisis realistically?

Are his priorities in order? Is he considering the needs of others, such as children?

5. **Personal Emotions**

What are his feelings?

Is he emotionally out of control?

Is he being led primarily by his emotions?

6. **Personal Behavior**

What is he doing?

Is he behaving responsibly?

7. **Personal Objectives**

What does the person want to accomplish?

What does he want you to do for him?

Are his goals or plans realistic and attainable?

8. **Personal Resources**

What resources does the person have?

Who can he call on for help?

Are there supportive friends, family, or neighbors available?

If this is a recurrent problem, how has he dealt with this problem in the past?

Are there social workers, pastors, counselors, or others already involved?

9. **Personal Responsibility**

Is the person willing to assume responsibility for the problem or for change?

What is his attitude toward and desire for real change? Is he willing to change his behavior and life-style, or is he simply wanting to be rescued or shown sympathy?

Is the person trying to manipulate you?

Is the person the victim of someone else's misbehavior and poor choices, or is the crisis the consequence of his own behavior or lack of action?

Will he make the commitment needed for change?

10. Professional Help

Can the person in crisis change this situation alone, or does he need to seek professional counseling or a rehabilitation program?

Is he already in counseling?

It is important to remember our limitations and refer people to professional counselors when appropriate.

Consider how the Helpline counselor who answered Jana's call used the questions in these ten areas as she helped Jana.

Jana called Helpline at eleven o'clock one cold winter night from a public telephone. She had been thrown out of a trailer where she had been living with a man named Joe.	**Precipitating Event**
She was very upset.	**Emotions**
Joe had pushed her around. But she was not physically injured.	**Physical Condition**
Standing beside her in the cold were two small children, but all she could talk about was her relationship with Joe.	**Behavior and Perception**
The telephone counselor had to let Jana talk about her relationship with Joe and allow her to vent her anger, before she could calm down and see that her real objective should be getting herself and her children to a warm place to spend the night.	**Presenting Problem**

Personal Objectives |

In helping her to assess her situation and the advisability of returning to the trailer, the telephone counselor learned that the woman had recently arrived in the community and was without family or friends for support.

Personal Resources

Jana agreed that she needed to get out of the cold weather. She had some money with her for cab fare, and the telephone counselor found shelter for her and the children at a Christian shelter for battered women where she could receive professional counseling.

Personal Responsibility

Professional Help

Presenting Problem, Real Problem

A person will often talk about a number of presenting problems. When he relaxes and begins to trust you because of your accepting, nonjudgmental attitude and approach, he will begin to open up and reveal more. Presenting problems are the tip of an iceberg. They are easily seen. But the larger, more serious problems are generally hidden beneath.

It is important to listen and accept the person and give him plenty of time to tell you about his problems. It may take a friend hours to finally be able to say, "I'm involved with a married man." Crisis counseling, like emergency surgery, requires a concentrated span of time. The amount of time needed is often longer than the regularly scheduled hour of long-term counseling.

RESPONSES THAT HELP

I mentioned earlier that we become more interactive in the second phase of the counseling model, asking questions and gently guiding the conversation. Let's look at the different types of questions you can ask and how you can use them in a counseling session.

Closed-ended Questions

If you begin by asking direct, or closed-ended, questions that call for a yes or no answer, the responsibility for solving the problem will shift to you. The burden will fall upon you to ask the "right" questions to determine what's wrong and to figure out how to "fix the problem." This is not the approach you want to use unless you are taking control, as in crisis intervention. In crisis counseling, you want to leave the control of the conversation with the counselee and reinforce the fact that he is responsible for solving his problem. You want him to open up and talk.

Direct questions often come across as clinical, cold, and distant. The person will answer one question, then wait for another. This may lead to his closing up or feeling pressured, like he is being interrogated.

Timing, tone of voice, acceptance, and compassion are important whenever asking questions. If answering your direct questions will be too revealing too soon, your friend may choose to lie. People do not respond well to a series of direct questions.

An appropriate time to ask a direct question is when you need a direct answer. A direct question is useful when confronting a problem or when a person seems evasive. The following are examples of direct questions:

"Bob, did you take the money?"

"Jane, have you started smoking?"

"Brenda, are you using drugs?"

As you can see direct, closed-ended questions come right to the point. They should be used very carefully.

The Pressure Question: Why?

Questions beginning with *why* can be particularly stressful for the person in crisis. "Why?" pressures the other person to explain his actions or behavior. Although it is appropriate to explore together some of the reasons for the behavior, asking "why?" can make people feel attacked because it is generally asked too quickly and too harshly. It can also encourage a person to shift blame rather than help him to slowly think through the situation and recognize his own responsibility or role in bringing about a desired change.

It is usually best to avoid using "why" questions altogether. But if you do use them, the same cautions and guidelines given regarding direct questions apply. Remember, your ultimate goal is to keep the person motivated to talk. Open-ended questions are particularly helpful for this.

Open-ended Questions

Open-ended questions cannot be answered with a simple yes or no. Instead, they place the control of the conversation in the hands of the person being questioned. Questions like "How did the accident happen?" "How do you feel about that?" "What options do you have?" give the other person the responsibility for talking and for exploring and resolving his own problem. The tone of voice you use to ask these questions is important, as it was with the closed-ended questions. Questions asked harshly, loudly, or in anger, invoke a different reaction from those asked quietly and gently!

Allowing the person in crisis to talk is in itself therapeutic for him. Getting it all out, telling his story, releases stress and tension and helps him to see the truth. Telling a story repeatedly helps him to better understand what happened. Open-ended questions can encourage this process.

Open-ended questions can also guide a person to explore or consider a given area. You may ask, for example, "What would happen if you took the job offer?"

Be careful not to push too hard or probe into embarrassing areas that a person may not yet be willing to reveal. This will cause him to withdraw and feel injured.

Open-ended Statements

Like open-ended questions, open-ended statements motivate a person to talk. They can be gently confronting, as with the statement, "It sounds as if you may be sexually involved with Pat." But they are less threatening than direct questions.

"Are you sexually involved with Pat?" is a direct question. It confronts the issue head-on. But it also concludes the discussion by calling for a yes or no response. The statement, on the other hand, keeps the conversation going because it is exploratory. It lets the person know that the helping friend is willing to discuss the possibility of the said behavior.

Open-ended statements are also called leading statements because they gently guide a person in a specific direction. This guiding technique takes the conversation into an area without deeply probing. The person is still in control of what is revealed.

Closed-ended and open-ended questions and statements are appropriate counseling responses, depending on where you are in the counseling interview and what you are trying to accomplish. They can be specifically applied in a technique called lending ideas, to help a person evaluate his resources and develop a plan of action.

LENDING IDEAS

Let's face it—nobody likes to be told what to do. Even people in crisis who are seeking counsel and advice really don't want to be told what to do. They want someone to listen to them and care. They want someone they trust to think things through with them, but in the end, they want to make their own decisions.

As we listen to people talk about multiple problems, we help them prioritize the problems and identify the one on which they need to focus. Then we *listen* while they talk about their options. Remember, while you are doing this, you must keep the responsibility on your friend or client to solve his problems. Don't offer advice. It is only after he has considered all of his available options and evaluated them, that you should begin to *lend* ideas for him to consider. Your client or friend must have ownership of the final decision or plan. After all, he will be the one to carry out his plan.

Lending ideas sounds something like this:

> *"I wonder . . . Some people in this position will do A-B-C. What do you think of A-B-C as an option? Are you familiar with X-Y-Z? Maybe that's a possibility?"*

The idea is that you want to bring ideas to the person's attention, for his consideration.

Watch out for the "Yes, but . . ." answer. For this person, nothing works short of giving him all your money. This is the "poor me" fellow who really does not want to develop a plan to work out his problem. Whenever you bring up an idea, he will say, "Yes, but . . ." and find something wrong with your ideas. He is the person in chronic crisis mentioned in chapter 1.

Plan Development

After guiding the conversation through the various options, you want to move the person toward plan development. This sounds something like the following:

> "Of all the options we've discussed, which seems the best to you?"
>
> "What do you think you should do today?"
>
> "What will be your first step?"
>
> "Where do you go from here?"

You will note that these questions leave the responsibility with your friend to make decisions and develop plans. As he responds to your questions, write his plan down and time-activate the steps: "Okay, let's see. You said you are going to do 1-2-3 by Friday. Let's get together on Monday and review your progress."

Be specific. Remember, objectives tell us how much and by when. Be careful not to lead a person too far, too fast. Set reasonable, attainable goals. Meet the person where he is, not where you think he ought to be.

If a person is at 3, don't ask him to go to 7. Instead, say, "Oh, I see, 1-2-3. What do you think you should do after 3?" If 4 is his idea, he will probably do 4, and you will have helped him. He is still not at 7, but you are making progress.

Counseling is a process. You are not going to get to 7 overnight. You start out by accepting him where he is at 3, then helping him to grow to 4 and beyond.

The next step is to ask him, "What do you think you will do after 4?" Perhaps he will respond by saying, "Well, maybe A or B." Accept his ideas as options. Discuss the advantages and disadvantages of A, as well as the advantages and disadvantages of B. Ask him if he has any other ideas, and when he says, "No," the time is right to lend other ideas: "I wonder what would happen if you tried 5?"

This technique requires patience. You are leading, not pushing or pulling. You are gently guiding your friend the way God guides you. Let's imagine you are counseling with Bill.

Bill is married and has two children. He has moved out of his house into an apartment "to have some time to think." Actually, he wants some time to be with his girlfriend.

Bill is talking to you about his financial problems, the demands his wife, Sandy, is placing on him, problems at work, and other issues. You know from counseling with Sandy that Bill has a girlfriend, but he has not told you of the affair.

It seems to you Bill lacks a relationship with Jesus. You have discussed his spiritual condition with Sandy, but Bill has not discussed the subject. He is agreeable to praying with you, though.

In short, you know Bill needs to go to 7. He needs to confess his sin of adultery, receive Jesus Christ as his Savior, break off the affair, and move back home with his wife and children. He needs to turn his life over to the Holy Spirit, pray, and go to church. He needs to give up his hard partying, drinking buddies and find some good Christian friends. You know what he needs: 7! A relationship with Jesus Christ! But that's not where Bill is. Bill is at 3.

Bill cannot see 7 right now, so you are going to have to meet him at 1-2-3. In the next section of our course, we will discuss how to lead a person into a relationship with Jesus Christ, how to confront his behavior, and how to help him change his behavior. But until your friend is ready for this relationship, as long as he remains at 3, you must meet him there. Indeed, you may pray that he reaches 7, but you must meet him at 3.

If your friend, like Bill, is blinded by lust, pleasure, alcohol, infatuation, the excitement that accompanies sin, you will have a longer, harder time in the counseling process. "No pain, no gain," the athletes say. The counselee must experience some pain before he will seek to change. He must recognize some problems before he will look for solutions or consider making changes.

Listen to his concerns; help him with the issues and problems of his concerns; and walk with him to 4 and 5. Help him overcome his denial (for Bill, life with his girlfriend is not perfect either) and recognize and deal with his problems. As you listen and accept the person, he will bond with you. When he tells you of his sins, remain unshockable. Don't pounce on the behavior; rather, continue to listen. Then, gently begin to explore the area of his sin, remembering how gently Jesus confronted the woman at the well.

The woman in chapter 4 who had a drug problem confirmed her desire to change her behavior and stop using drugs. Her last words were, "Can you help me?" Watch how the counselor focuses on her problem and helps her establish a plan using the responses we've discussed. Notice how the counselor does not jump in and push her beyond where she is. He meets her at 1-2-3 and slowly walks with her as she reaches the answer.

LEADING AND PLAN DEVELOPMENT

Counselor:	"What have you done so far to get off the drugs?"	**Open-ended Question**
She:	"I've thrown away my pipes and flushed drugs down the toilet, but I always go back and buy more."	
Counselor:	(pause) "What else have you tried?"	**Open-ended Question**
She:	"I started going to Narcotics Anonymous."	
Counselor:	"Narcotics Anonymous?"	**Content Response**
She:	"Yes, they have meetings every night. I don't always go. It's good for people who have already made the break, but . . ."	
Counselor:	(pause) "What other options do you have?"	**Open-ended Question**
She:	"My mother wants me to go into a drug program."	
Counselor:	"I see." (pause)	**Conversational Response**

	"How do you feel about that?"	Open-ended Question
She:	"I'm afraid I'd lose my trailer and my furniture."	
Counselor:	"You're afraid you'd lose your trailer and furniture?"	Mirror Response
She:	"Yes—a drug program costs a lot of money and it would take all I have."	
Counselor:	"I see. (pause) If you did lose your trailer and your furniture, could they be replaced?"	Conversational Response Closed-ended Question: Used to Confront
She:	"Yes, maybe, but I've got to have something to come back to."	
Counselor:	"You took out a mortgage on the trailer and spent all the money on drugs. (pause) How are the mortgage payments going?"	Summarizing Open-ended Question
She:	"I'm behind. (pause) I guess I'm going to lose the trailer anyway, huh?" (pause)	
Counselor:	(pause) "What are you thinking?"	Open-ended Question
She:	"I should go into the drug program!"	

In the problem-solving phase, you should try to focus on one problem at a time. Sometimes the person in crisis is confused and dealing with multiple problems. Let him meander, but once he has identified various problems, help him to focus on one problem until he resolves that, and then move on to the next.

In this case study, the woman realized she had a drug problem and needed help, but she was afraid of losing her trailer. She was helped to see that her trailer was already lost. At that point, she was ready to take the next step and go into the drug program. The process is like climbing a staircase—taking each problem one step at a time.

As counselors and helping friends, we want to be like the Wonderful Counselor, who is described by words such as gentleness, peace, patience, self-control. Jesus also was firm, confronting sin, which we will need to be at times. But the primary personality of the Christian counselor/friend is loving, accepting, nonjudgmental—walking with the person. We do have a direction to lead the person: to Jesus Christ. We do have an absolute, guaranteed-to-work, perfect guidebook—the Bible. In Part Two of our course, we will turn to the Bible even more as we focus on our spiritual counseling model.

Select one of the role plays from the following list. Have one person take the part of the counselor and one person play the role of the person in crisis. Feel free to expand on these examples or to make up other situations.

Each role play counseling session should last ten minutes. As you do the role play, use the responses we've studied: mirror, conversational, content, feeling, open-ended questions, leading statements, and guiding responses. Do not expect to solve the problem in the time allotted. When your ten minutes are up, reverse roles and select another situation.

Role Plays

Steve, 22.

"I really don't know what I want to do with my life. I am about to graduate from college. Nancy wants to get married. But I'm kind of frightened by it all.

"I think we ought to wait until I have a job and I have saved some money. She's afraid we will drift apart. Our relationship is beginning to heat up sexually, and I want to put on the brakes before it goes too far."

Martha, 50.

"I'm divorced. My husband left me for a younger woman.

"My kids are all grown, and they have adjusted to the divorce well. They say, 'Mom, you've got to live for yourself now.'

"All my life, I've been a housewife and mother. Now, I don't have my house; I'm not a wife; and the kids are grown. How do you start over when you're 50?"

Krissie, 25.

"I'm a schoolteacher, but I don't think I can take it anymore. Three of my fourteen-year-old students got pregnant this year. I think a boy in one of my classes is a drug dealer. One of my students got in a fight at school and pulled a knife on another student.

"The government has messed up our school system so badly. The administration won't back you up when you need to discipline a student. Parents don't care.

"I just want out, but I'm not trained to do anything else. I'm really frustrated."

Jack, 19.

"I can't find anybody. There are a couple of girls that hang around at school, but I'm not really interested in them. The girls

I'm interested in just want to be friends. It's like I'm a nice guy, but nobody wants to care."

Tom, 43.

"My daughter didn't come home last night. She's 17. My wife and I are separated, and Susie was staying with me for the weekend. I let her use my car to be with her friends, but she didn't come home.

"She left Friday. This is Sunday afternoon, and I don't know where she is! Surely, she's all right. Her mom is going to kill me."

Becky, 33.

"I'm afraid to be alone. I was raped last year by a friend of my husband. I have never told anyone. I just didn't believe it happened. I was in shock and he kept telling me that if I said anything nobody would believe me. I don't ever see him or anything, but I'm afraid to be alone. My husband doesn't understand what's going on, and I can't tell him."

Gary, 45.

"I got fired from my job and I haven't told my wife. It's crazy. It's like I don't want to believe that it happened. I keep thinking I'll wake up. It's a horrible nightmare.

"I have a son in college and we haven't saved any money. The weekend is almost over. I guess I'll have to . . ."

Jerry, 19.

"I'm really in trouble. I had a wreck. Nobody got hurt, but the car is banged up.

"I'm a student at college and I'm afraid my father will find out. Maybe if I can get a part-time job, I can earn the money to fix the car. I was . . . drinking, and I can't let my dad find out. He's a minister."

Esther, 62.

"I just got the news that my sister died. She was going in for some light surgery and her heart just couldn't take it. I can't believe it. We have always been so close."

Sonya, 14.

"My mom's boyfriend comes into my room at night when she's sleeping. When she first started dating him, I thought he was cute. We'd all do things together—go to the beach and stuff. Then he moved in with my mom. I woke up one night and he was touching me. I'm really scared.

"I can't say anything. He's been coming in every night and touching me. I don't know what to do."

Cathy, 32.

"I got home tonight from work and my husband's things were gone. He called me a few minutes ago and said he has moved out. He wants a divorce. I don't know what to do. There must be another woman.

"For years, I've been looking the other way. I just never thought he . . . he would dump me."

EXERCISE
Open-ended Questions

Open-ended questions often begin with what, where, or how: *What* have you done so far to solve this problem? *Where* are you going today? *How* do you feel about that? Open-ended questions stimulate conversation and help people to focus on issues.

Write an open-ended question as your Group Leader reads one of the following statements. Then, in turn, each person in the group can read his question. Complete the exercise responding to one statement at a time.

For Example:

Young Man: I don't know whether to take the promotion and continue working, or quit and go back to school.

Counselor: What would be the advantage of going back to school?

1. **Man:** I've tried to find a job. I just can't find anything.

   _____
   _____
   _____

2. **Young Girl:** Bob has asked me to marry him.

   _____
   _____
   _____

3. **Girl:** I'm at my wit's end.

   _____
   _____
   _____

4. **Woman:** My boss said that I will have to move to Albany if I want to get into the training program.

_____

_____

_____

5. **Man:** What do you think I should do?

_____

_____

_____

Give completed exercise to Small Group Leader.

HOMEWORK
Chapter 5

Name _____

Date _____

Group Leader _____

Write the requested response to the following statements.

1. **Woman:** Seems like everything I do is wrong.

   Mirror Response: _____

   _____

   _____

2. **Secretary:** This guy is just impossible to work with. He dumps piles of work on my desk and walks off. He doesn't seem to realize that I work for two other people in the office. I could just cry. It didn't used to be this way.

   Conversational Response: _____

   _____

   _____

3. **Ex-Convict:** I've been looking for a job, but when they find out I just got out of jail, that's it. They won't give me a chance.

   Content Response: _____

   _____

   _____

4. **Young Woman:** I think I've finally found some people I can relate to. I went to the singles group that you suggested. They were really nice. I felt like they accepted me.

Feeling Response: _____
_____
_____

5. **Businessman:** The company is in debt and they have fired lots of people. They say I can stay, but I'll have to go on straight commission—no salary.

   Open-ended Question: _____
   _____
   _____

6. **Patient:** Nobody's told me a thing. They took the tests this morning. I'm just lying here. The nurses won't tell me anything and I haven't seen the doctor.

   Feeling Response: _____
   _____
   _____

7. **Young Girl:** I don't know how it happened. I just dropped it. It was my grandmother's favorite vase, and I just dropped it.

   Content Response: _____
   _____
   _____

8. **Man:** He just called on the phone and fired me. No warning, no nothing!

   Rephrase: _____
   _____
   _____

9. **Teenage Girl:** I just want to die. All of a sudden I'm pregnant and my boyfriend acts like he doesn't even know me!

   Content Response: _____
   _____
   _____

10. **Elderly Woman:** Nobody cares about me. They don't call or write. They have their own lives now.

    Feeling Response: _____

    _____

    _____

    Give completed homework to Group Leader at your next class.

CLOSING DEVOTION
Road to Emmaus
Luke 24:13–35

Let's take a walk down the road to Emmaus with Jesus. It is the first Easter Sunday as Jesus comes alongside two of His disciples. Observe the Master's active listening techniques and His use of open-ended questions.

READER ONE
SCRIPTURE PASSAGE

READER TWO
OBSERVATIONS

1. "Now behold, two of them were traveling that same day to a village called Emmaus, which was about seven miles from Jerusalem. And they talked together of all these things which had happened. So it was, while they conversed and reasoned, that Jesus Himself drew near and went with them. But their eyes were restrained, so that they did not know Him.

2. Jesus came alongside and walked with the men. Counseling can take place in any location.

Now, watch how Jesus motivated the men to talk with an open-ended question.

3. "And He said to them, *'What kind of conversation is this that you have with one another as you walk and are sad?'*

4. *Jesus used active listening.*

5. "Then the one whose name was Cleopas answered and

READER ONE SCRIPTURE PASSAGE	READER TWO OBSERVATIONS
said to Him, 'Are You the only stranger in Jerusalem, and have You not known the things which happened there in these days?'	6. *Jesus accepted the men* even though in their grief, their responses to Him were rather rude and curt.
7. "And He said to them, 'What things?'	8. *He motivated them to talk with another open-ended question.* Jesus knew "What things." He was simply using this active listening response to stimulate the conversation.
9. "So they said to Him, 'The things concerning Jesus of Nazareth, who was a Prophet mighty in deed and word before God and all the people, and how the chief priests and our rulers delivered Him to be condemned to death,	10. As they talked, *Jesus listened.*
11. and crucified Him. But we were hoping that it was He who was going to redeem Israel. Indeed, besides all this, today is the third day since these things happened. Yes, and certain women of our company,	

READER ONE
SCRIPTURE PASSAGE

who arrived at the tomb early, astonished us. When they did not find His body, they came saying that they had also seen a vision of angels who said He was alive. And certain of those who were with us went to the tomb and found it just as the women had said; but Him they did not see.'

13. "Then He said to them, 'O foolish ones, and slow of heart to believe in all that the prophets have spoken!

15. 'Ought not the Christ to have suffered these things and to enter into His glory?' And beginning at Moses and all the Prophets, He expounded to them in all the Scriptures the things concerning Himself.

17. "Then they drew near to the village where they were going, and He indicated that He would have gone farther.

READER TWO
OBSERVATIONS

12. Notice how the grieving disciples talked and talked as *Jesus listened.*

Jesus listened to these loved ones who were in crisis.

14. *Jesus confronted them.* Gentle confrontation is needed at times to help people to see that they are going in the wrong direction.

16. *Jesus taught them.* Teaching and sharing ideas can be an important part of the personal counseling process.

18. *Jesus did not force Himself* on these men.

READER ONE SCRIPTURE PASSAGE	READER TWO OBSERVATIONS
19. "But they constrained Him, saying, 'Abide with us, for it is toward evening, and the day is far spent.' And He went in to stay with them.	20. *He established a strong relationship* with the men. They wanted Him to continue. *Jesus gave up control* over the relationship. When they sought Him, *He responded to them in a warm way,* meeting them for dinner.
21. "Now it came to pass, as He sat at the table with them, that He took the bread, blessed and broke it, and gave it to them. Then their eyes were opened and they knew Him;	22. *He revealed Jesus, the Christ,* to them.
23. and He vanished from their sight.	24. Once the counseling need had been met, *the counseling relationship was terminated.*
25. "And they said to one another, 'Did not our heart burn within us while He talked with us on the road, and while He opened the Scriptures to us?'	26. The men reflected on what had happened.

READER ONE SCRIPTURE PASSAGE	READER TWO OBSERVATIONS
27. "So they rose up that very hour and returned to Jerusalem,	28. They changed their direction.
29. and found the eleven and those who were with them gathered together,	30. They sought out the Body of Christ, the church.
31. saying, 'The Lord is risen indeed, and has appeared to Simon!' And they told about the things that had happened on the road, and how He was known to them in the breaking of the bread."	32. They shared what Jesus had done for them.

Isn't it exciting to see that the active listening skills, open-ended questions, and other counseling principles being studied in this course were used by Jesus two thousand years ago?

Closing Prayer

Chapter 6

HELP Solve the Problem: Part II

The counseling responses we have learned can be used in various ways to guide and direct our clients or friends. The conversational, the mirror, the content, the feeling responses will become a part of our normal communication skills throughout the counseling process.

Our responses to clients or hurting friends can also be directive, guiding, confronting. We need to be aware of how our responses can be used to affect the counseling process.

Silent Response

At times in the counseling process a person will stop talking. He may be collecting his thoughts or reflecting on what has been said. It is important that you sit there and be quiet. Be still. Don't move around.

Being silent with a person communicates love. In the silence you share an intimate moment. Your willingness to be quiet lets the person know that you care. By not putting pressure on him to say something, to fill the silence, you allow him to release his tension. Perhaps the Holy Spirit is speaking to him. It is important, therefore, to be quiet and allow the Holy Spirit to minister.

Sometimes people try to conclude a conversation following a period of silence. If your client/friend tries to do this, simply reflect a leading statement, like, "Tell me more about . . ." and he will be off talking again. This time, however, he will be less tense and able to think more clearly.

Feeling Response

As we said in chapter 3, people in crisis are often directed by their feelings. Thus, allowing them to express their feelings may prevent them from doing something foolish. Now that we've studied open-ended responses, let's look at some examples of how you can use open-ended statements and questions to help motivate a person to talk about his feelings.

"How did that make you feel?"	**Open-ended Question**
"You are really mad."	**Reflect Feeling**
"I know you must be disappointed."	**Leading Statement**
"Tell me how you feel."	

Directive Response

Content responses can be used to take the conversation a certain direction. These are called directive responses.

Whatever you reflect back to a person tends to direct the conversation to that subject because the person usually responds to what you say. Therefore, it is important that you reflect back the area perceived as causing the person the greatest concern or the area upon which you feel the person needs to focus. For example, a person calling you on the phone may say, "He said he doesn't love me and he just walked out. I don't know where he is." You can respond, "You don't know where he is?" and thereby focus the conversation on his physical location. However, it is even better to respond, "He said he doesn't love you?" and direct the conversation to that area of their relationship.

Summary Response

Summarizing the main points of what a person has said helps everyone better understand a situation. As you re-present the ideas in an orderly and chronological manner, you and the person in crisis will be able to reconsider the most important points of what has been said. Thus, the person will perhaps see his situation more clearly or realize that he may have left something important out of his story.

Summarizing can also be used in leading and directing the conversation. If a person has told his story and is beginning to repeat himself, summarizing is a good way to perhaps conclude the discussion of one area and move on.

Rephrasing Response

Rephrasing is restating what the person has said in your own words. The following is an example of a rephrasing response.

Person: "I failed Chemistry and I'm going to be on probation next quarter. When my dad finds out, he's going to kill me."

Counselor: "You think your dad will really be upset when he finds out about your grades."

Rephrasing is not simply repeating the person's words, but rather saying what you think the person means. It slows down the conversation because the other person must listen to what you are saying. But it helps the person to rethink what he is saying. Be careful, however. If you rephrase too much, the person who is talking may feel like he is being analyzed rather than listened to.

Empathetic Response

Sympathy is different from empathy. If you express sympathy, you actually take on the feelings of another person. *Empathy* is understanding what a person's situation is like and *feeling with* him, but remaining objective and not taking on his emotions.

We are most helpful as counselors if we remain objective. Consider the difference in the responses in these illustrations.

You are at home with your husband when he receives a phone call. His father has suddenly died. You and your husband grieve together. His feelings are your feelings. You are a *sympathetic* wife. Months later, a friend at work receives a phone call. Her father has suddenly died. You sit with her in the conference room while she weeps. You do not cry, but you care and put your arm around her. You are her *empathetic* counselor. There is a time and a place for empathy and sympathy.

Realistic Response

Sometimes the person in crisis struggles in a state of denial; he is not very realistic about his situation. A Christian man may leave his wife for another woman, for example. The Christian wife, who was left, may pray and hold on to the belief that God will bring her husband back to her.

God promises to answer prayer, but this does not mean He will overpower a person's free will, even when the person is choosing a sinful path. In the case of the abandoned wife, reconciliation may not be a realistic possibility. You will want to offer hope, but you cannot do this by supporting unrealistic expectations. Instead, you must gently lead the wife to consider all possibilities.

Confronting Response

As Christians, we are to be accepting and nonjudgmental. This means we love all people regardless of how they act. Being nonjudgmental means that we do not judge or condemn a person. This does not mean that we should accept all behavior as appropriate.

As we discussed in chapter 2, secular psychology lacks the biblical guidelines found in Christian psychology. Without these moral guidelines, secular counselors are not able to confront sinful behavior, and they even become accepting of it. They do not work in harmony with the Holy Spirit to help people to lead new and transformed lives. Thus, secular counselors deal with the area of confrontation differently from Christian counselors.

As Christian counselors and friends, Jesus is our model counselor. We want to observe how Jesus confronted people and follow His example. Jesus loved the sinner but confronted sinful behavior. So must we!

As helping friends, we have to be careful not to come on too strong as the Great Authority or Instant Analyst. If we stand on the mountain and talk down to our hurting friends, or if we moralize at them, we will not reach them. Notice how gentle Jesus was with the woman caught in adultery (see John 8). He accepted her. And because He accepted her, she was able to call Him Lord. Then Jesus said, "Go and sin no more."

God's Word says we should "put on tender mercies, kindness, humility, meekness, longsuffering" (Col. 3:12). We have to set aside our ego and pride and try not to be Super Hero who solves the problem. It is much better to come down off the mountain and meet hurting people where they are, struggle with them, confront them, and help them discover the right answers for themselves.

If you are in a class, choose two members to role play the following case as the rest of the class observes. If you are on your own, you may want to find a friend who will act this out with you. Look for the mistakes this counselor is making. Consider how you would respond differently. Discussion questions follow the drama.

The Counseling Process

Counseling can be defined as a process beginning with a time of listening and moving to a time of reflecting, then exploring, and finally, resolving.

LISTENING: "Uh huh . . . I see . . . OK . . . Yes . . . Sure . . . Tell me more about it." Remember the need for periods of silence in the conversation. These are called growth gaps.

REFLECTING: "You feel . . . think . . . believe . . . What I hear you saying is . . ."

EXPLORING: "How do you feel when . . . ?"
"What do you see as the main problem?"
"What alternatives do you have?"

RESOLVING: "What do you think is your best option?"
"What are you going to do first?"
"How do you think you should proceed?"

THE RENT'S DUE

Counselor: This is Helpline. May I help you?

Caller:
(female) Yes! I've got a problem! The rent's due and I don't have any money. I'm afraid my landlady is going to kick me out. (pause)

Counselor: Your rent's due (pause) and you don't have any money.

Caller: I was sick last week and missed three days of work. I didn't get paid much. I gave my landlady a check thinking I could get the money from my sister, but she said she can't give it to me right now. She said she could give me some money on Friday, but I need the money now.

I don't want to do anything bad for it, (pause) but I need the money now. (pause) My land-lady said she kicked out the girl who lived here before me because she didn't pay the rent. Can you help me?

Counselor: I'll try. Let me see if I understand. Your rent's due and you don't have the money.

Caller: That's right.

Counselor: You gave your landlady a bad check and . . . (cut off)

Caller: (tense) I was going to cover it!

Counselor: I understand. You were going to borrow the money from your sister to cover the check you gave your landlady.

Caller: Yes.

Counselor: But, you can't get the money until Friday and you're afraid your landlady will cash the check, discover it's no good, and kick you out of your apartment.

Caller: I just have a room, but yes, that's it.

Counselor: How much is your rent?

Caller: Seventy-five dollars a week.

Counselor: You mentioned having a sister. Do you have any other family in the area?

Caller: No, just my sister.

Counselor: How often are you paid?

Caller: Each week.

Counselor: What about getting an advance on your paycheck?

Caller: It's a new job. I've only been working there two weeks.

Counselor: What about the job before that?

Caller: He wouldn't loan me any money.

Counselor: What about the people you used to work with? Do you think any of them might lend you some money?

Caller: Maybe. I don't know. I don't want to go back there!

Counselor: What about talking with your landlady?

Caller: She'll kick me out.

Counselor: She's going to be angry when she cashes your bad check.

Caller: Yeah.

Counselor: And, you will have a $20.00 or $30.00 bank charge.

Caller: (silent)

Counselor: You're in a tight spot. You've made some bad decisions and the consequences are not good. You're going to have to do something you don't want to do. You're going to have to talk to your landlady.

It's better not to surprise her. If you explain things to her, she won't kick you out.

Caller: You don't know her!

Counselor: Well, could you give her something? How about part of the rent?

Caller: I don't have any money.

Counselor: What about church? Have you talked to your pastor about this?

Caller: (tense, loudly) I don't want to talk about God right now! I spent two months living on the streets in New Jersey with nobody to help me. I can't go back to that! (hang up)

Case Review

What mistakes did the counselor make? Discuss the following questions in your group, or write your thoughts in response to the questions in the space provided.

1. How did the counselor do moving through the first phase of the counseling model? Did the counselor listen long enough? Did he focus on the person? Or did the counselor move too quickly into problem solving?

_____

_____

_____

_____

_____

2. What did the counselor identify as the problem? Was this the presenting problem or the real problem?

_____

_____

_____

_____

_____

3. Concerning the presenting problem, did the counselor help the caller to identify and explore her options and resources?

_____

_____

_____

_____

_____

4. What kind of help did the caller expect to receive from the counselor? Did the counselor clarify the type of assistance or help the caller could expect to receive?

_____

_____

_____

_____

_____

5. How did the counselor help the caller to explore her options? What open-ended questions did the counselor use to draw the caller into talking about her situation or exploring her options?

_____

_____

_____

_____

_____

6. How did the counselor use active listening to help relieve the caller's anxiety?

_____

_____

_____

_____

_____

7. Was the counselor patient?

_____

_____

_____

_____

_____

8. What is an example of the counselor's promising the caller something he could not guarantee?

_____

_____

_____

_____

_____

9. Did the counselor lead the conversation into the spiritual area too quickly or too abruptly?

_____

_____

_____

_____

_____

10. What were some of the positive points the counselor attempted or achieved?

_____

_____

_____

_____

_____

11. Was the counselor correct in attempting to help the caller to see her responsibility and need to discuss the matter with the landlady? How could this have been accomplished more successfully?

_____

_____

_____

_____

_____

Now let me give you the rest of the story.

The Rest of the Story

The young woman who called is named Nancy. She is twenty-one years old.

Nancy's stepfather sexually abused her and her sister, Carol, for years. Nancy's mother was addicted to alcohol and drugs as the girls grew up. She worked from time to time as a bartender in New Jersey.

Nancy and Carol finally ran away from home. Nancy ended up working the streets as a prostitute. When her boyfriend (pimp) beat her up one day, she hitched a ride with a long-haul trucker to Florida. In return for her transportation, she granted him sexual favors. (Nancy has a venereal disease.)

Nancy worked a few weeks as a nude dancer in Tampa, but left after seeing a girl, strung out on drugs, being beaten up by her pimp. Nancy ran to Orlando where she rented a room from the landlady mentioned in the call. She found a job at a local retail store as a cashier. When she called Central Florida Help-line, she had been sick and missed work, and was low on cash.

Did the counselor blow it? Did the counselor do a horrible, unforgivable job? Are things like this going to happen to us if we serve as telephone counselors or get involved in trying to help people?

The counselor tried to help the caller but he moved through the counseling model too quickly and he was too directive. He was also too judgmental.

In evaluating this call, we also need to remember that every problem is not going to be resolved satisfactorily. We are not professional counselors, and we are going to make mistakes. (By the way, professional counselors make mistakes too.) But even when we do everything right, we will find that some situations are unsolvable. The pain and the consequences cannot be avoided. The people we help may continue to choose the wrong way or avoid dealing with their problems. We cannot take responsibility for solving their problems. We will be very frustrated if we do.

Instead of trying to become Super Counselor, we must remember that there is a Wonderful Counselor. When a call ends abruptly or when a caller refuses to acknowledge problems or work on solutions, we must remember that the Wonderful Counselor will go on with him. The Lord has used us for a brief period. He will now lead that person to someone else through whom He will work.

The counselor in this example did make some counseling errors. He didn't listen and let the caller be in control of the conversation. He took control and began asking a lot of questions, trying to solve the problem right away. He led the conversation into the spiritual area abruptly. He also promised things he couldn't guarantee. But God worked in spite of the errors.

Two days after Nancy hung up on the counselor, she called back and talked to another counselor. Nancy had talked to her landlady as the first counselor had suggested. The landlady agreed to hold Nancy's check until Friday. The presenting problem was solved.

The second counselor used her active listening skills to discover the underlying problems we've just discussed. Nancy enrolled in a Teen Challenge program and has been there for several months. She recently dedicated her life to Jesus Christ, and her life is beginning to come together.

MAKING REFERRALS

Sometimes a person needs to be under the care of a professional counselor or enrolled in a specialized program, such as a residential treatment center. It is not a sign of failure or inadequacy for us to refer a person to someone else or to some other program or agency for help. As helping friends, we can be bridges for people to the specialized counselors or programs they need. We can utilize the various community directories available through our local government, telephone crisis center, or other agencies, and network with the many sources of help in the community.

We need to be a part of this network and make referrals when appropriate. But it is important not to make referrals early in the counseling interview. A person may interpret our making referrals too early in the conversation as rejection, an uncaring attitude, or a refusal to provide help. There are exceptions, of course, particularly, when a person is specifically seeking referral information and does not want to talk. In such instances, provide the information requested.

Take time now to role play with a partner from your small group, practicing a counseling situation. Choose someone with whom you have not previously role played and make up your own crisis situation. When you have finished, switch roles with your partner and repeat the role play.

CLOSING DEVOTION
Personal Ministry

The word *laity* is not in the Bible. It was never the plan of God that the minister should minister while the congregation congregates. All believers have been called to be priests (Ex. 19:6; 1 Peter 2:5, 9; Rev. 1:6). The power of the Church of Jesus Christ will only be released in the world when Christian laypeople assume their role and responsibility as priests.

The wonderful thing about our calling into personal ministry is that we are not alone. Jesus said, "I will ask the Father, and he will give you another Counselor to be with you forever" (John 14:16 NIV), and "You shall receive power when the Holy Spirit has come upon you" (Acts 1:8). It is the Holy Spirit who ministers, comforts, and counsels through us as we yield to Him.

We have been called and we have been chosen to be His disciples. He will prepare us for personal ministry, and He will perform that ministry through us as we yield to Him. The days ahead are going to be *exciting!!*

Closing Prayer

Chapter 7

Put the Counseling Responses into Practice

You have acquired a number of new counseling skills. Now it's time to put those skills into practice. In this chapter you will be able to participate in a complete counseling session. You will be able to experience the role of the counselor and of the counselee. If you are studying this with a group of people divide into groups of two, and read the following counseling interview. *Read the interview straight through.* This will give you a feel for the actual counseling session. *Then go back and identify the counseling response that was used, filling in the blanks.*

Sue called Christian Helplines at 11:00 P.M. Her exchange with the counselor follows.

Counselor: This is the Helpline. May I help you?

She: I . . . I hope so . . .

Counselor: What seems to be the problem?

Response: _____

_____

_____

She: It's my husband. (crying) He is so insensitive and uncaring.

Counselor: (pause) I see.

Response: _____

_____

_____

She: I told him I was thinking about a divorce.

Counselor: Uh, huh.

Response: _____

_____

_____

She: (crying) And he just walked out of the room.

Counselor: He just walked out of the room?

Response: _____

_____

_____

She: Yes!

Counselor: (long pause) When did the problem first start?

Response: _____

_____

_____

She: Oh, three months ago, I had my baby, Theresa. She was two months early and we were afraid she was going to die. It has been touch and go for the last three months.

First she was in the preemie ward of the hospital and I was with her 16 hours a day. Ralph, my husband, travels, and after the first week, he had to go back on the road. I was all alone. My mother is dead. Ralph's mother and father came over for a week, but they had to leave and then I was all alone. We're new to the area.

Ralph would come home at odd times between trips. It's the season and he had to be out in the trade shows on weekends, and then calling on customers during the week. I understand all that, but then the baby came home, and there was all that medical equipment in our bedroom for the baby. Ralph said he couldn't sleep with all that stuff and he moved out into the den at night.

I was looking after the baby twenty-four hours a day, (pause) but, things are better now. Theresa is going to be all right. The equipment is gone. She's sleeping through the night. (pause) Ralph is back in the bedroom, when he's home! (pause)

Counselor: I see. (pause)

Response: _____
_____
_____

What seems to be the problem now?

Response: _____
_____
_____

She: (crying) They want me to go away and leave Theresa.

Counselor: (long pause) Who is they?

Response: _____

_____

_____

She: My husband and the doctor.

Counselor: Your husband and the doctor want you to go away . . .

Response: _____

_____

_____

She: Yes, and leave Theresa!

Counselor: Where do they want you to go?

Response: _____

_____

_____

She: On a vacation someplace!

Counselor: I see, and you don't want to go.

Response: _____

_____

_____

She: No! I don't want to leave my baby!

Counselor: You don't want to leave your baby.

Response: _____

_____

_____

She: No.

Counselor: Tell me about your baby's condition.

Response: _____

_____

_____

Is everything O.K. now? Is she healthy and stable?

Response: _____

_____

_____

She: (pause) Yes.

Counselor: Let me see if I understand this. Three months ago you had a little girl, Theresa.

Response: _____

_____

_____

She: That's right.

Counselor: Theresa was born premature and you were afraid she was going to die.

Response: _____

_____

_____

She: Yes.

Counselor: For the past three months, you and your husband have been under a lot of pressure, and you are both very tired. Am I right?

Response: _____

_____

_____

She: Uh huh.

Counselor: Now, your husband and your doctor are recommending that you go away on a vacation.

Response: _____
_____
_____

She: That's right.

Counselor: Do you think your husband wants what is best for you?

Response: _____
_____
_____

She: I guess.

Counselor: Are you tired?

Response: _____
_____
_____

She: Yeah, I really am!

Counselor: Who could stay with the baby if you and Ralph went away for a few days?

Response: _____
_____
_____

She: My mother-in-law could probably stay.

Counselor: You mean Grandma?

She: (laughing) Yeah, Grandma.

Counselor: You think Grandma knows anything about babies?

Response: _____

_____

_____

She: Yeah, well, she had four of her own, and she has six grandkids.

Counselor: Sounds like she's had lots of experience.

Response: _____

_____

_____

She: Yeah.

Counselor: You feel like you need to get some rest?

Response: _____

_____

_____

She: Yeah, I really do.

Counselor: And a few days off with Ralph would help?

Response: _____

_____

_____

She: Yeah.

Counselor: Let me ask you about what you said earlier, about a divorce . . .

Response: _____

_____

_____

She: I didn't mean it.

Counselor: But, you said it.

Response: _____
_____
_____

She: Yeah.

Counselor: How do you think your husband feels right now?

Response: _____
_____
_____

She: I'm not sure. (pause) Maybe a little hurt.

Counselor: How do you feel about your husband?

Response: _____
_____
_____

She: I love him.

Counselor: Where is he now?

Response: _____
_____
_____

She: He's in bed.

Counselor: Is he asleep?

Response: _____
_____
_____

She: I don't think so.

Counselor: What do you think about going and getting in bed with your husband, and saying you're sorry . . .

Response: _____

_____

_____

She: I think that's a good idea.

Counselor: . . . and telling your husband you realize you both need to get away, and you love him?

Response: _____

_____

_____

She: I can handle that.

Counselor: How do you feel now?

Response: _____

_____

_____

She: Much better.

Counselor: You think the vacation is a good idea?

Response: _____

_____

_____

She: Yeah. I always did. I just didn't want to leave my baby.

Counselor: But, you are over that fear now.

Response: _____

_____

_____

She: Yes, I think so.

Counselor: Could we pray together?

Response: _____

_____

_____

She: Sure.

Counselor: Heavenly Father, we thank you for Theresa. We thank you for Sue and Ralph who love her and each other so very much! We ask you to bless their marriage and their time away together.

Let this vacation be a time of peace and rest. Watch over Theresa and her grandma, we pray. Keep them safe while Sue and Ralph are on their vacation. These things we pray in Jesus' name, Amen.

She: Amen. Thank you.

Counselor: Sue, where do you go to church?

Response: _____

_____

_____

She: Well, we haven't been going.

Counselor: I see. Where did you used to go?

Response: _____

_____

_____

She: A long time ago, I was a Baptist. I was raised a Baptist.

Counselor: I see. Tell me more about your personal beliefs.

Response: _____
_____
_____

She: I believe in Jesus and all, you know. I've just been away so long. I did a lot of praying when Theresa was sick.

Counselor: And you believe God answered your prayers?

Response: _____
_____
_____

She: I know He did.

Counselor: What would you gain by finding a church near you and joining a young couples class?

Response: _____
_____
_____

She: I guess we'd make a lot of friends.

Counselor: Does that sound like a good idea?

Response: _____
_____
_____

She: Sure does. We just haven't gotten around to it.

Counselor: Are there any churches near you?

Response: _____
_____
_____

She: Yeah, there is a Baptist church about six blocks away.

Counselor: What's the name of the church?

Response: _____
_____
_____

She: Glendale Baptist.

Counselor: Would it be all right if we asked the pastor or a young couple from Glendale Baptist to call on you?

Response: _____
_____
_____

She: Oh sure, but make it after we get back from our vacation.

Response: _____
_____
_____

Counselor: O.K. Tell me your last name.

Response: _____
_____
_____

She: Jenkins.

Counselor: And your address?

She: 909 Glen Court.

Counselor: And your phone number?

She: 982-7676.

Counselor: O.K. Go tell your husband you love him, and plan your vacation.

She: I will. Thank you for your help! I feel so much better. You have helped me so much!!

Counselor: I'm glad. (pause) God bless you.

She: God bless you too. Good night.

Counselor: Good night.

HOMEWORK
Chapter 7

Name _____

Date _____

Group Leader _____

Most people have never taken the time to write down their testimony. The story of your relationship with God, however, can be a strong tool when attempting to tell someone about Jesus Christ. People are more interested in what God has done in the lives of real people than in theology.

The homework assignment is to write out your testimony. Keep it short, three to five minutes. Discuss:

1. What your life was like before you met Jesus Christ and His Holy Spirit;

2. When and how you committed your life to Christ;

3. What your life has been like since.

Rewrite and edit your testimony until it is smooth. Practice giving it several times by yourself, and then to a close friend or family member. Be brief and to the point. Don't dwell on the past or emphasize how bad you used to be. Don't get technical or theological. And don't try to recruit people to your church. Don't miscommunicate that Christians are perfect people or that becoming a Christian will solve all of a person's problems.

Instead, keep your testimony simple, light, and open. Ask the Holy Spirit to guide you, and write it down to hand in to your Small Group Leader during Class Nine.

In the classes ahead we will study evangelism and spiritual counseling. To be adequately prepared you need to memorize the following:

1. Learn to recite your three- to five-minute testimony.

2. Memorize the Sinner's Prayer (see below) word for word.

3. Memorize the two diagnostic questions, adapted from Dr. D. James Kennedy's book *Evangelism Explosion* (used by permission).

Sinner's Prayer

1. Lord Jesus, I need You.

2. Thank You for dying on the cross for my sins.

3. Forgive me for my sins, I pray.

4. I turn away from my sins right now,

5. And, receive You as my personal Savior.

6. Send Your Holy Spirit to live within me.

7. Take control of my life.

8. Make me the kind of person You want me to be.

Diagnostic Questions

1. "Have you come to the place in your spiritual life where *you know for sure* that if you were to die tonight, you would go to heaven?"

2. "Let's suppose that it happened. You were in an automobile accident and killed. You were called to stand before God and He said to you, 'Why should I let you into heaven?' What would your answer be?"

The Lord will help you memorize these questions and prayers. It is imperative that you be prepared when someone is ready to receive Christ. Memorize these and God will use you to bring many friends and loved ones to salvation. These are the tools of a disciple.

CLOSING DEVOTION

As Christians, we have a role model in Jesus Christ, the Wonderful Counselor.

THE GREATEST COUNSELOR

In John 4:7–42 (NIV), we observe Jesus as He counseled a Samaritan woman at a place called Jacob's Well. Jesus had sent His disciples into town for food and sat down near the well to wait. It was about 6:00 P.M. when footsteps could be heard.

"When a Samaritan woman came to draw water, Jesus said to her, 'Will you give me a drink?' . . .

"The Samaritan woman said to him, 'You are a Jew and I am a Samaritan woman. How can you ask me for a drink?'"

The social and religious customs of the day dictated that Jesus not speak to a woman, much less a Samaritan woman.

Samaria was a ghetto for Jews who intermarried with heathen tribes. A purebred Jew would have nothing to do with a Samaritan half-breed. Jesus was a holy man. She was a sinful woman. But Jesus pushed aside all prejudice and asked her for a drink, indicating a willingness to drink from a common cup with her. He then led the conversation from the physical to the spiritual. "Jesus answered her, 'If you knew the gift of God and who it is that asks you for a drink, you would have asked him and he would have given you living water.'

"'Sir,' the woman said, 'you have nothing to draw with and the well is deep. Where can you get this living water? Are you greater than our father Jacob, who gave us the well and drank from it himself, as did also his sons and his flocks and herds?'" The woman pointed out their common ancestor, Jacob.

"Jesus answered, 'Everyone who drinks this water will be thirsty again, but whoever drinks the water I give him will never thirst. Indeed, the water I give him will become in him a spring of water welling up to eternal life.'" Jesus revealed Himself as the source of the living water and promised that it would give eternal life. And though the woman did not comprehend what He was saying, she asked for what Jesus had to offer.

"'Sir, give me this water so that I won't get thirsty and have to keep coming here to draw water.'"

Jesus then gently confronted the woman's sinful behavior and lifestyle. "He told her, 'Go, call your husband and come back.'

"'I have no husband,' she replied.

"Jesus said to her, 'You are right when you say you have no husband. The fact is, you have had five husbands, and the man you now have is not your husband. What you have just said is quite true.'" Jesus knew that the woman was not married, but He wanted to allow her to confess her sin. He led the conversation into the area of her sin so she could confess it.

"'Sir,' the woman said, 'I can see that you are a prophet. Our fathers worshiped on this mountain, but you Jews claim that the place where we must worship is in Jerusalem.'" Jesus responded to her spiritual question, "'Believe me, woman, a time is coming when you will worship the Father neither on this mountain nor in Jerusalem. You Samaritans worship what you do not know; we worship what we do know, for salvation is from the Jews. Yet a time is coming and has now come when the true worshipers will worship the Father in spirit and truth, for they are the kind of worshipers the Father seeks. God is spirit, and his worshipers must worship in spirit and in truth.'"

Then the woman professed her faith in the coming

Messiah. "The woman said, 'I know that Messiah' (called Christ) 'is coming. When he comes, he will explain everything to us.'

"Then Jesus declared, 'I who speak to you am he.'"
Jesus revealed Himself more directly to this obscure Samaritan woman than He did to His own disciples. The woman left her jar immediately and went back to town, telling the people to come out and see the man "who told me everything I ever did." Was this the Christ? she wondered.

The Samaritans followed her to Jesus. Many of them believed in Him because of the woman's testimony. And others believed because they heard Jesus speak Himself.

Jesus set an example at the well for all Christian counselors.

1. He reached out to the woman and cared about her.

2. He accepted her. Jesus did not judge or criticize her because of her social or religious status or her sinful behavior and life-style. Indeed, He made her aware that He knew her life-style. But He continued to show her respect and valued her as a person in talking with her.

3. He was patient with the woman, listening to her and showing empathy for and understanding of what she had to say.

4. He gently confronted her sin. He allowed her to discuss her behavior and confess her sin.

5. Finally, He revealed Himself, the Messiah, to her. Jesus was concerned about the woman's eternal life. And when He revealed Himself, she went and told others about Him.

In the next section we will learn how to spiritually counsel with people; how to introduce people to Jesus in a gentle, nonthreatening way; how to confront sinful behavior; how to effectively share our testimony.

Many people came to believe in Jesus because of the Samaritan woman's testimony.

Closing Prayer

Personal Evangelism

PART TWO

*We proclaim him, admonishing and teaching
everyone with all wisdom, so that
we may present everyone perfect in Christ.*

Colossians 1:28 (NIV)

Chapter 8

*LOVE Them to Christ: Part I, The Home Run Presentation**

In the second part of this course we will look at our calling as disciples of Jesus Christ. When Jesus first called His disciples, He held out His arms and said, "Come, follow me, . . . and I will make you fishers of men" (Mark 1:17 NIV). In one brief statement, our Lord said three important things.

First, He said, "Come." A person must first come into a personal relationship with Jesus Christ as his Savior.

Then, Jesus said, "follow me." Once a person has come to Christ, he must follow the Holy Spirit as Lord of his life.

Finally, Jesus said, "I will make you fishers of men." When the Holy Spirit is in control, the person can claim the wonderful promise that Jesus will make him His disciple.

---

*The two diagnostic questions and the Sinner's Prayer used in the Home Run Presentation of the Gospel have been adapted, with permission, from Dr. D. James Kennedy's *Evangelism Explosion* and Dr. Bill Bright's "Four Spiritual Laws," respectively. The Christian world is most indebted to these two men for their leadership and development of training materials in the area of Christian evangelism.

So far in this course, we have looked at the first two phases of the personal counseling model, which has been reprinted for you below. We have learned to minister to the *person* in crisis and help him with his *problem*. Now we turn our attention to the person's spiritual life, his *personal relationship* with God, as we apply the techniques of the third phase of the counseling model.

PERSONAL		SPIRITUAL		
PERSON	PROBLEM	PERSONAL RELATIONSHIP	PERSONAL BEHAVIOR	PERSONAL MINISTRY
ARMS	HELP	LOVE	CARE	CHRIST

Only when a person enters into a personal relationship with Jesus Christ can his sins be forgiven. Only by surrendering his life to the lordship of the Holy Spirit can a person find the power to live a new and transformed life.

As Christian counselors, or helping friends, we become fishers of men when we reach out to hurting friends and help them come into a personal relationship with Christ. In order to do this we employ the techniques of the word picture LOVE:

L —*Lead* the conversation into the spiritual area;

O —*Offer* God's love and plan of forgiveness and salvation through Jesus Christ; offer whatever spiritual counseling and support is needed.

V —*Verify* the power and presence of the Holy Spirit, once the person has prayed to receive Christ; and

E —*Encourage* the person into the fellowship of a local Bible teaching church.

The Three Strikeout Prayers

Anytime we lead conversations toward spiritual things, we engage in spiritual warfare. So before we begin to talk with people about their relationship with Jesus Christ, we need to pray and bind Satan from interfering.

Here are three strikeout prayers you can fire off to do this:

Strike One: Ask God to convict the person of his sins.

Strike Two: Ask God to reveal the truth of Jesus Christ to the person.

Strike Three: Ask God to give him the faith to believe.

A person will not come to Christ because of our slick salesmanship or presentation. He will come because the Holy Spirit has convicted him of his sins (John 16:8), revealed the truth to him (John 14:26), and given him the faith to believe (Eph. 2:8). If the person is receptive and willing, God will reach him through you.

Now that you have prayed these prayers, you are ready to begin.

L: *LEAD* THE CONVERSATION INTO THE SPIRITUAL AREA

In making the transition into the spiritual area, we want to be sure we do not come on too strong. Allow the other person to do most of the talking and use open-ended questions to direct the conversation. It all comes together something like this:

Counselor: "A lot of times, people with problems like this will talk to their pastor. Have you talked with your pastor about this?"

Man: "No. I don't really have a pastor."

Counselor:	"I see. Are you attending a church at the present time?"
Man:	"No, I'm not."
Counselor:	"Tell me about earlier in your life. When you were a child, what kind of church did your family attend?"
Man:	"Well, my mother was a Baptist. She was very religious. My father didn't go to church much. Mom took us to church when we were small, but when we got to be teenagers, we kind of stopped going."
Counselor:	(pause) "Tell me about your personal beliefs today."
Man:	"Oh, I believe in God if that's what you mean. I just don't believe you have to go to church."
Counselor:	"I see."
Man:	"I can get a lot closer to God out on the golf course on Sunday morning than I can by attending some meeting."
Counselor:	"I understand. Let me ask you a question."
Man:	"Sure."
Counselor:	"Have you come to the place in your spiritual life where you know for sure that if you were to die tonight that you would go to heaven?"

Encourage the person to talk about his beliefs and his religious background. The conversation may become more involved than this example, but don't be drawn into a deep spiritual discussion or debate. Let the person talk about spiritual things long enough to become relaxed and comfortable with the subject. Finally, direct the conversation into a presentation of the Gospel. Begin with the two diagnostic questions.

For the smoothest transition into these questions, ask permission to ask them. The counselor above did this by saying, "Let me ask you a question."

The Two Diagnostic Questions

In his book *Evangelism Explosion,* Dr. D. James Kennedy presents two diagnostic questions that effectively lead conversations into a presentation of the Gospel and reveal a person's religious beliefs. With Dr. Kennedy's permission, I have slightly adapted the two questions for this text.

The counselor in the previous example asked the first question: "Have you come to the place in your spiritual life where you know for sure that if you were to die tonight that you would go to heaven?" Memorize the question exactly as presented here. It has been carefully thought out and is effective for several reasons. Let's break it down.

> **"Have you come to the place in your spiritual life."** This opening phrase acknowledges that the person has a spiritual life. You are not putting him down. You are also acknowledging that his spiritual life is in a process of growth.

> **"Where you know for sure."** That's the hook—knowing for sure. Your goal is to help the person be certain of and secure in his spiritual life.

> **"That if you were to die tonight."** This phrase intellectually brings the person to the point of his death. It stresses the urgency of the question—that there is an immediate need for an answer.

"That you would go to heaven?" Now, you have the person thinking about what will happen after his death.

After asking this question, sit back and listen. Let the person open up and talk. Again, this is not the time for a theological discussion or debate.

Once the person has responded, move on to the second question. Again, gently take control of the conversation, politely asking permission to ask another question: "Let me ask you another question. Let's suppose that you were involved in a traffic accident and killed. You are called to stand before God, and He says to you, 'Why should I let you into heaven?' What would your answer be?"

How does this direct the person with whom you are talking?

"Let's suppose that you were involved in a traffic accident and killed." Automobile accidents are a fact of life; they are realistic possibilities. Notice the question is worded so that the person cannot object to your supposition—it is a possibility even if the person does not drive.

"You are called to stand before God." The story brings the person beyond the point of death to where he is facing God.

"And He says to you, 'Why should I let you into heaven?' What would your answer be?" The answer to this question will reveal what the person is trusting for his salvation. If the question had been, "Do you know Jesus?" or "Are you a Christian?" there would still be some uncertainty about the person's beliefs, even after he answered. A lot of people can answer questions identifying who Jesus is. But these people may not be trusting in the atoning sacrifice of Jesus Christ for their salvation.

After asking each of the diagnostic questions, remain silent. You have led the conversation into the spiritual area. Now, allow the other person to do most of the talking.

We don't want people to feel as though we are preaching at them. Instead, they need to be able to verbalize their thoughts and beliefs. If we allow them to do this, they will be more receptive when we begin to share the Gospel.

Typical non-Christian responses to the second diagnostic question include,

"No, I don't think I will go to heaven. I haven't lived a very good life."

"Yes, I think I will go to heaven. I go to the Catholic, Baptist, etc., church."

"Yes, I think I will go to heaven. I help people. I've never killed anybody."

A lot of people believe that living a moral life and doing good works will get them to heaven. If you do not hear the person make a clear reference to the fact that Jesus died for our sins and that he has a relationship with Jesus Christ, then you need to present God's plan of salvation. The person may know who Jesus is and still not know Jesus as his Savior.

The specific presentation of the Gospel you are asked to learn is called the Home Run Presentation of the Gospel. There are several good presentations of the Gospel, but for our study, I ask students to memorize the Home Run Presentation. It has been tremendously effective used over the telephone, as well as face to face.

O: *OFFER* GOD'S LOVE AND PLAN OF FORGIVENESS AND SALVATION THROUGH JESUS CHRIST

In the game of baseball, there are four bases. To score a run, a person must hit the ball and run safely to first base, then to second, past shortstop to third, and finally home. Visualizing a baseball diamond, review the following basic steps in leading a person into a personal relationship with Jesus Christ:

First Base: We have all sinned, haven't we?

Second Base: What's the penalty for sin?

Shortstop: There was a time in my life, when I heard people saying that the penalty for sin is death or that Jesus died for my sins, and I didn't understand that. Can you explain that to me?

Third Base: Restaurant Story

Home Run: Sinner's Prayer

Memorizing this brief outline will help you as you learn the details of the presentation.

First Base: We Have All Sinned, Haven't We?

The first thing a person must do is admit he is a sinner. You can gently guide him to agree with this through your response to his answer to the second diagnostic question.

To the person who does not believe that he will go to heaven, you can say, *"Sounds like there are some things in your life that you know you should not have done, but then, nobody's perfect. We have all sinned, haven't we?"* To the person who believes that he will go to heaven because he has been good, you may respond, *"Sounds like you have tried to live a good life. Of course, nobody's perfect. We have all sinned, haven't we?"* In either case, you are leading the person to agree that "we have all sinned," thereby admitting, "Yes, I am a sinner too."

Emphasizing the *we* in your question is a nonthreatening approach to helping a person through this stage. When he has admitted that he too has sinned, he has arrived at first base. Now you are ready to discuss the penalty of sin.

Second Base: What Is the Penalty for Sin?

You reach second base by asking the open-ended question, "What is the penalty for sin?" After you ask this, listen. The responses will vary: "Hell"; "Death"; "I don't know." Allow the person to talk. But again, don't be sidetracked into a discussion or debate. Instead, keep moving to shortstop.

Shortstop: I Didn't Understand. Can You Explain?

Lead the person to shortstop with the question, "There was a time in my life when I heard people saying that the penalty for sin is death, or that Jesus died for my sins, and I didn't understand that. Can you explain that to me?" This gives the person an opportunity to explain his understanding of God's plan of salvation. When you acknowledge that you once did not understand, you identify with the person and let him know it is all right if he does not understand. If the person does not express an understanding of God's plan of salvation through Jesus Christ at this point, move on to the Restaurant Story.

Third Base: Restaurant Story—Jesus Paid for Me

At third base, you want your friend or counselee to come to an understanding that Jesus died in payment for our sins. The following story illustrates this point:

I'd like to share a story with you that has explained a lot of things for me.

Suppose I invite you out to eat as my guest. While we are in the restaurant, the waitress comes over and says there is an emergency phone call for me. So I go to the telephone.

A moment later, I return, saying, "There has been an accident. My father is at the hospital and I need to leave right

*away." You respond, "Certainly, I understand. I hope
everything is going to be all right." Then, I leave.*

*You continue to sit there, eating alone, when you
suddenly realize you don't have any money with you. I had
invited you out to eat, so you had not brought any.*

*You finish eating and go to the counter, where the
manager is standing. You tell the manager, "I certainly
enjoyed my meal, but I . . . uh, I don't have any money with
me."*

*The manager gets a big smile on his face and says,
"That's okay, your friend paid for you before he left."*

*All you have to do at this point is accept the fact that I've
paid for you, and you can walk out of the restaurant—free.*

*That's how it is with us. You and I have sinned. The
penalty for sin is death. But God loves us so much that He
came in the person of Jesus, died on the cross, and paid for
our sins. He paid for us. And all we have to do is accept the
payment He made.*

After you have told this story, present the Sinner's Prayer.

Home Run: Sinner's Prayer—Pray to Receive Christ

Without hesitation, move to home plate with the following
prayer. This "Sinner's Prayer" is a slight variation of that which
appears in the Campus Crusade for Christ International booklet
"Four Spiritual Laws," written by Dr. Bill Bright.

Begin by saying, "Listen carefully to these words. They are
the words of a prayer:

Lord Jesus, I need You.
Thank You for dying on the cross for my sins.
Forgive me for my sins, I pray.
I turn away from my sins right now.
I receive You as my personal Savior.

Send Your Holy Spirit to live within me.
Take control of my life.
Make me the kind of person You want me to be.

Would you like to pray this prayer with me right now?"

Wait quietly for an answer. Don't move around. If the caller or person you are with says he would like to pray, then repeat the prayer. Your friend should repeat each line after you say it, as shown below:

Counselor: Pray aloud after me. Lord Jesus, I need You.

Caller: Lord Jesus, I need You.

Counselor: Thank You for dying on the cross for my sins.

Caller: Thank You for dying on the cross for my sins.

Continue through the prayer to the end.

When you have finished the prayer, don't say anything. Wait quietly and let the Holy Spirit minister to your friend. A life of sin and guilt has just been lifted from his shoulders. He has just been spiritually born; the Holy Spirit of God has entered into him. Some people will cry, some will glow, and some will just be quiet for a moment.

Repeating the Sinner's Prayer *before* asking him to pray it, helps the person to better understand the step he is being asked to take. If you simply ask, "Do you want to pray and receive Christ?" the person will not really understand what he is committing to.

Imagine a man standing outside the door of a dark room. Another man stands at the door and motions the first gentleman, saying, "Come in." The first man may be apprehensive about entering. After all, he can't see what is ahead of him. If the second man at the door turns on the light and then invites the first man to come into the room, the first man's apprehension will lessen. He can now see what is before him and understand where he is going.

Take a close look at the steps involved in inviting a person to pray the Sinner's Prayer:

"Listen carefully to these words." This statement gets the person's attention.

"These are the words of a prayer." This identifies the words that follow as a prayer.

"Lord Jesus, I need You . . ." By saying the words of the prayer and then inviting the person to pray, you are "lighting the room." If the person says he would like to pray, ask him to repeat aloud each line of the Sinner's Prayer.

If the person responds, "No, I don't think so, not right now," respect his position but do not terminate the presentation. Instead, try to understand his objections and answer his questions so you can help him to go ahead and take that all-important step of surrendering his life to Jesus Christ. Give the person a second opportunity to pray the Sinner's Prayer. Do not stop with the first no.

What Happens When You Get Off-track?

Sometimes the people we counsel take the conversation off into "left field" by asking legitimate questions or raising objections. They may ask, for example, "Why does God allow bad things to happen to good people?" or "What is God going to do with the heathen?" These are legitimate questions, but Satan can use these as stumbling blocks to stop the Gospel presentation.

The best way to handle this situation is to allow the person to express his question and admit that it is important. Help the person with whom you are talking understand that even mature

Christians have problems understanding some of these questions. Write the question down and agree to come back to it later. Then proceed with the presentation.

A presentation of the Gospel should not be a high-pressure presentation. No one can push or pull another person into heaven. God is seeking a relationship with each individual in which the person surrenders his life freely. Therefore, we must respect the objections of those to whom we present the Gospel. We need to listen to them and give them the opportunity to express their thoughts and feelings.

People may need to ventilate anger and resentment regarding how the church or Christians have hurt them in their past. As we listen in love, we can share our witness as to what God has done in our own lives. We may share how we, too, have been hurt and disappointed by people. As we gently respond to people, they become more open to receiving the truth we are presenting. The Scripture says, "Quietly trust yourself to Christ your Lord and if anybody asks why you believe as you do, be ready to tell him, and do it in a gentle and respectful way" (1 Peter 3:15 TLB).

Allow the conversation to meander a little or the person to raise objections. But unless the person is not receptive at all to hearing the presentation, bring the conversation back on track.

After the person has received Christ, you can verify to him that the Holy Spirit is present in his life.

V: *VERIFY* THE INDWELLING OF THE HOLY SPIRIT

In the following conversation, the counselor verifies that the Holy Spirit is living within him now that he has accepted Jesus Christ as his Savior. The interchange between the counselor and the caller will give you an idea of how you can instruct someone who has just received Jesus Christ as his Savior.

Counselor:	You know, perhaps you didn't just see lightning or hear thunder, but I want to assure you with the promise of God that His Holy Spirit has just come into you and He will never leave you. In your Bible, turn to the 14th chapter of John and read verse 16.
Caller:	"And I will ask the Father, and he will give you another Counselor to be with you forever" (NIV).
Counselor:	For how long?
Caller:	Forever.
Counselor:	Jesus promised to send His Holy Spirit to live in us forever. Now read verse 26.
Caller:	"But the Counselor, the Holy Spirit, whom the Father will send in my name, will teach you all things and will remind you of everything I have said to you" (NIV).
Counselor:	Who is our teacher?
Caller:	The Holy Spirit.
Counselor:	And what will He teach you?
Caller:	All things . . . Wow!
Counselor:	Now turn to Galatians, chapter 5, and read verses 16 to 23.
Caller:	"I say then: Walk in the Spirit, and you shall not fulfill the lust of the flesh. For the flesh lusts against the Spirit, and the Spirit against the flesh; and these are contrary to one another, so that you do not do the things that

you wish. But if you are led by the Spirit, you are not under the law.

Now the works of the flesh are evident, which are: adultery, fornication, uncleanness, lewdness, idolatry, sorcery, hatred, contentions, jealousies, outbursts of wrath, selfish ambitions, dissensions, heresies, envy, murders, drunkenness, revelries, and the like; of which I tell you beforehand, just as I also told you in time past, that those who practice such things will not inherit the kingdom of God.

But the fruit of the Spirit is love, joy, peace, longsuffering, kindness, goodness, faithfulness, gentleness, self-control. Against such there is no law."

Counselor: God promises that if we allow His Holy Spirit to control our lives, we will not be overcome by the sins that used to control us. Instead, His Holy Spirit will bring forth love, joy, peace, patience, kindness, goodness, faithfulness, gentleness, and self-control. These are the things in life that we are really looking for aren't they?

Caller: Yes, they are.

Counselor: That does not mean that we won't continue to have problems. But it does mean that we will never be alone again and that He will help us to overcome our problems.

After you have walked someone through these Scripture passages, you can encourage him or her to join a local fellowship of believers.

E: *ENCOURAGE* INTO THE FELLOWSHIP OF THE LOCAL CHURCH

When people we counsel or talk with choose to follow Christ, it's not time to carve a notch in the Bible and walk away! God gives us the wonderful privilege of being part of the birth of new Christians. Those baby Christians then need some special attention and guidance while they grow into maturity. One thing we can do to help in that process is encourage them to join a local church.

When you do this, use open-ended questions to find out if your friend already goes to a church:

Counselor: Tell me, where have you been going to church?

Caller: Well, I haven't been going.

Counselor: I see. Are there any churches near your house?

For a detailed conversation, in which the counselor discusses the caller's church, look back to chapter 7.

You can ask a local church to call on your new Christian friend. Or if you are meeting with a person, face-to-face, you can even invite the person to attend church with you. You can also see that he obtains a modern translation of the Bible; introduce him to Christian friends; meet with him periodically; pray with him; teach and share.

We need to be willing to walk further with people after we lead them to Christ. This is all part of the process Jesus called us to when He said, "Go and make disciples" (Matt. 28:19 NIV) and when He told us He would make us "fishers of men" (Matt. 4:19 NIV).

PLAY BALL!

No pitcher strikes everyone out. No team wins every game and not all people will pray to receive Christ, no matter how skillful our presentation. We do not have to feel guilty if, after making a presentation, people elect not to pray and receive Christ. We cannot save anyone. Only the Holy Spirit can convict people of their sin, reveal the truth of Jesus, and give them the faith to believe. God is ready to respond when people are willing to receive. As Christ's disciples, however, we must share the Gospel with those around us, regardless of the results.

At times we will break new ground, at times we will plant or water, and at times we will be blessed by participating in the harvest and birth of a new Christian or assist in the rededication of a person's life. It is our responsibility to share. It is the Lord's role to save.

Take time now to practice the two diagnostic questions, the Home Run Presentation, and the process of verifying the presence of the Holy Spirit. Find a partner and take turns reading the counselor's part and the caller's part of the dialogue that follows.

This portion of the counseling interview illustrates the third phase of the counseling model. At this point, the counselor has led the conversation into the spiritual area. He is now ready to ask the first diagnostic question.

EXERCISE
Presentation

Counselor: Let me ask you a question.

Caller: Okay.

Counselor: Have you come to the place in your spiritual life where you know for sure that if you were to die tonight that you would go to heaven?

Caller: I don't know. I think so.

Counselor: Let's suppose that it happened. You were in an automobile accident and killed. You are called to stand before God, and He says to you,

"Why should I let you into heaven?" What would your answer be?

Caller: I don't think God would ask that question.

Counselor: You're probably right. (pause) Let's just suppose He did. If you were standing before God, and He did say to you, "Why should I let you into heaven?" what would your answer be?

Caller: I was raised a Christian. I help people when I can. I give to the church.

Counselor: Sounds like you've tried to live a good life. Of course, nobody's perfect, right?

Caller: No, that's for sure.

Counselor: We have all sinned, haven't we?

Caller: Yes.

Counselor: Tell me, what is the penalty for sin?

Caller: Hell, I guess.

Counselor: You know, there was a time in my life when I heard people say, "The penalty for sin is death," or that Jesus died for my sins, and I didn't understand that. Can you explain that to me?

Caller: No, not really.

Counselor: I heard a story once that helped explain some things for me. Let me share it with you. Let's suppose that I invite you to meet me at the Pancake House. I'm going to buy breakfast. We meet and while we are eating our pancakes, the waitress calls out my name to pick up a phone call. I go to the telephone and come back to say that a friend of mine has been in an accident. He's at the hospital and I need to leave right away. You say that you hope everything is going to be all right. We agree to meet another day, and I disappear out the door.

You are sitting there enjoying your pancakes when all of a sudden you realize you didn't bring any money with you. I was the big spender who was going to buy breakfast, and I had just run out the door!

You finish eating your pancakes and go up to the counter. The manager is standing there. You explain about not having any money and, he gets a big grin on his face and says, "That's okay, the man who was with you paid for you before he left."

You see. All you would have to do is accept the fact that I had paid for you and you could walk out of the restaurant free. That's how it is in life with us. You and I have sinned. The penalty for sin is death. Yet God loved us so much that He came in the person of Jesus Christ and He died in payment of our sins. All we have to do is accept that He paid for us, and we can be free.

Listen carefully to these words. These are the words of a prayer:

Lord Jesus, I need You.
Thank You for dying on the cross for my
    sins.
Forgive me for my sins, I pray.
I turn away from my sins right now and
    receive You as my personal Savior.

Send Your Holy Spirit to live in me.
Take control of my life.
Make me the kind of person You want
me to be.

Would you like to pray this prayer with me,
right now?"

Caller:	Yes, I would.
Counselor:	Okay, I'll pray first. Then you pray aloud after me. Lord Jesus, I need You.
Caller:	Lord Jesus, I need You.
Counselor:	Thank You for dying on the cross for my sins.
Caller:	Thank You for dying on the cross for my sins.
Counselor:	Forgive me for my sins, I pray.
Caller:	Forgive me for my sins, I pray.
Counselor:	I turn away from my sins right now,
Caller:	I turn away from my sins right now,
Counselor:	and, receive You as my personal Savior.
Caller:	and, receive You as my personal Savior.
Counselor:	Send Your Holy Spirit to live within me.
Caller:	Send Your Holy Spirit to live within me.
Counselor:	Take control of my life.
Caller:	Take control of my life.
Counselor:	Make me the kind of person,
Caller:	Make me the kind of person,
Counselor:	You want me to be.

Caller:	You want me to be.
Counselor:	In the name of Jesus, Amen.
Caller:	In the name of Jesus, Amen.
Counselor:	(Remain silent)
Caller:	(pause) Thank you.
Counselor:	I'm glad I was here. Do you have a Bible nearby?
Caller:	I think I know where one is.
Counselor:	What about a pen and a piece of paper?
Caller:	I can manage that. (pause) I'm back.
Counselor:	Turn to the book of John in the New Testament, chapter 14.
Caller:	Ahh, Matthew, Mark, Luke, John—got it, chapter 14.
Counselor:	This is the Last Supper where Jesus promised to send His Holy Spirit. Read verse 16.
Caller:	"And I will ask the Father, and he will give you another Counselor to be with you forever" (NIV).
Counselor:	For how long?
Caller:	Forever.
Counselor:	Jesus said that God would send us another Counselor and He would be with us forever. God has sent His Holy Spirit to live in you and He will never leave you. Now, read verse 26.
Caller:	"But the Counselor, the Holy Spirit, whom the Father will send in my name, will teach you all

things and will remind you of everything I have said to you" (NIV).

Counselor: Who will teach us?

Caller: The Holy Spirit.

Counselor: The Holy Spirit will teach us! We can have a close, personal relationship with the Holy Spirit of God, but . . . we must talk to Him through prayer. We must listen to Him through meditation. We must read what He has written to us as we study the Bible. We must worship Him in church.

Turn to the book of Galatians. It's over about four books toward the back. Acts; Romans; Corinthians; and Galatians.

Caller: I've got it!

Counselor: Chapter 5, verse 22. Read it for me.

Caller: "But the fruit of the Spirit is love, joy, peace, longsuffering, kindness, goodness, faithfulness, gentleness, self-control. Against such there is no law."

Counselor: When the Holy Spirit is in control of our life, He will produce this kind of fruit in us.

Now, switch roles and repeat the exercise. Practice this presentation until you can give it smoothly.

HOMEWORK
Chapter 8

Continue to prepare a three- to five-minute personal testimony:

1. State what your life was like before you met Jesus Christ and His Holy Spirit;

2. When and how you committed your life to Christ;

3. What your life has been like since.

   Memorize: the Two Diagnostic Questions, the Home Run Presentation of the Gospel, John 14:16, John 14:26, Galatians 5:22.

Practice the Home Run presentation of the Gospel several times before the next class.

CLOSING DEVOTION
Jesus and Nicodemus
John 3:1–17

READER ONE: The meeting between Jesus and Nicodemus is one of the most revealing and important meetings in all of history. Nicodemus was one of seventy men who served on the Sanhedrin, the ruling council of the Jewish people. Two years following his meeting with Jesus, Nicodemus spoke out on Jesus' behalf before the Sanhedrin. And after the crucifixion of Jesus, Nicodemus and Joseph of Arimathea were the ones who prepared and buried the body of Jesus. Listen as we read of this historic meeting found in John 3:1–17.

READER TWO: "There was a man of the Pharisees named Nicodemus, a ruler of the Jews. This man came to Jesus by night and said to Him, 'Rabbi, we know that You are a teacher come from God; for no one can do these signs that You do unless God is with him.'"

READER ONE: Under cover of darkness, this Jewish leader had come to see Jesus. He was aware of the miracles that Jesus was performing and that only someone in close communion with God could do these things. Jesus came right to the point:

READER TWO: "Jesus answered and said to him, 'Most assuredly, I say to you, unless one is born again, he cannot see the kingdom of God.'"

READER ONE: Nicodemus didn't understand. "'How can a man be born when he is old? Can he enter a second time into his mother's womb and be born?'"

READER TWO: "Jesus answered, 'Most assuredly, I say to you, unless one is born of water and the Spirit, he cannot enter the kingdom of God. That which is born of the flesh is flesh, and that which is born of the Spirit is spirit.'"

READER ONE: When a man is born, the water in his mother's womb breaks and he is born of water. Flesh gives birth to flesh. For spiritual birth to occur, the Holy Spirit of God must enter man. Spirit gives birth to spirit. In the Bible, whenever we read Spirit with a capital "S" the reference is to the Holy Spirit of God. When we read spirit with a small "s" the reference is to the spirit of man. It is when a person confesses his sin, repents, receives Jesus Christ as his personal Savior, and asks the Holy Spirit of God to come into him that a person is "born again" and receives spiritual life from God.

READER TWO: And Jesus said, "'Do not marvel that I said to you, "You must be born again." The wind blows where it wishes, and you hear the sound of it, but cannot tell where it comes from and where it goes. So is everyone who is born of the Spirit.'"

READER ONE: "Nicodemus answered and said to Him, 'How can these things be?'"

READER TWO: "Jesus answered and said to him, 'Are you the teacher of Israel, and do not know these things? Most assuredly, I say to you, We speak what We know and testify what We have seen, and you do not receive Our witness. If I have told you earthly things and you do not believe, how will you believe if I tell you heavenly things? No one has ascended to heaven but He who came down from heaven, that is, the Son of Man who is in heaven. And as Moses lifted up the serpent in the wilderness, even so must the Son of Man be lifted up, that whoever believes in Him should not perish but have . . . everlasting life. For God did not send His Son into the world to condemn the world, but that the world through Him might be saved.'"

READER ONE: **Closing Prayer**

Chapter 9

LOVE Them to Christ: Part II, The Power of Personal Testimony

"But you shall receive power when the Holy Spirit has come upon you; and you shall be witnesses to Me in Jerusalem, and in all Judea and Samaria, and to the end of the earth."

The Last Words of Jesus Christ
Acts 1:8

In His last words, before ascending into heaven, Jesus called us to be His witnesses. He then sent His Holy Spirit to live in us, to empower us to be His witnesses. Clearly, we have been called to be witnesses for Christ Jesus.

What does a witness do? He gives his testimony. A person's testimony is a powerful thing. Juries and judges listen to the testimonies of people and, on the basis of those testimonies, decide if a person on trial is to live or die.

I remember when I first became a Christian. I told *every-body* about Jesus. I even witnessed to the mailman, I was so excited and on fire.

I am still excited and on fire, but I have since learned to contain my enthusiasm and share Jesus, the Home Run Presentation, and my testimony when other people are receptive to hearing it. The personal counseling model shows that there are typically several steps we must go through before people are ready to talk about Jesus Christ or spiritual things. We need to meet the people where they are, put our ARMS around them, provide HELP for the problem, and then—maybe—they will be open to receiving our testimony or allowing us to guide them in the Home Run Presentation of the Gospel.

Back when I was just on fire and excited, I witnessed to a lot of people, but I can't remember reaching anyone. My witness was not effective. Now that I allow the Holy Spirit to control me, the fire is a warmth that draws people to Jesus. The excitement is a joy in the Lord that people want in their life. With His help, I have learned when and how to be a witness for Christ.

TAKE THE GOSPEL TO THE ENDS OF THE EARTH

When we are not counseling but simply meeting people—on airplanes, at bus stations—and talking and getting to know one another, we will often have opportunities to witness. Second only to airplane flights, I find lunch most productive for sharing a testimony. I have shared my testimony and led people to the Lord in pancake houses and restaurants all across America. In the next chapter is a presentation of the Gospel called the Two Triangles, which is ideal to use in restaurants.

In witnessing it is important to invest in the other person first. Listen to him; take an interest in him. Whether you are on an airplane or having lunch at a restaurant, build a relationship with the other person. Let him talk about himself first. Use active listening skills to draw him out. You may find that God has placed you beside this person for a very special reason. I have sat beside Christians who were flying home for a parent's or friend's surgery, and I was able to bring the Lord's comfort and peace to them. This may happen to you.

When the time comes for you to talk, you can use your testimony as a "lead-in" to a presentation of the Gospel. Share the greatest story:

- About what your life was like before you met Jesus Christ;

- About where and how you turned your life over to the Lord; and

- About what your life has been like since.

It's easy to talk about yourself. In fact, the hard part is not to talk too much. That's why you need to get your testimony down to three to five minutes. You still need to get through the Home Run Presentation and back to work on time.

It is exciting to share what God has done in your life and then lead a person to Jesus Christ. Remember, the person of the Holy Spirit is flowing through you to that other person. It is the Holy Spirit who convicts the person of his sin. It is the Holy Spirit who reveals the truth of Jesus Christ to a person. It is the Holy Spirit who gives him the faith to believe. It is the Holy Spirit who chooses to work through you as you witness to those around you. Fear not, for He is with you.

Take time now to form groups of three and share your testimony. Be sure to turn in your written testimony to your group leader.

CLOSING DEVOTION
The Great Commission
Matthew 28:18–20

Meditate on these verses. Talk with others about what this means to you, or write your reflections.

> *And Jesus came and spoke to them, saying, "All authority has been given to Me in heaven and on earth. Go therefore and make disciples of all the nations, baptizing them in the name of the Father and of the Son and of the Holy Spirit, teaching them to observe all things that I have commanded you; and lo, I am with you always, even to the end of the age."*

Closing Prayer

Chapter 10

LOVE Them to Christ: Part III, The Two Triangle Presentation

Many times we find ourselves counseling with a Christian who has fallen into some sinful behavior. The Two Triangle Presentation is effective in helping this person understand who God is, who he is, and how he can relate to God in overcoming his sinful behavior. This is an extremely important presentation. With it you can help friends overcome alcoholism, smoking, drug addiction, sexual immorality, and many other negative behaviors.

Two Triangles show you how to change your thoughts, your desires, and your behavior. We will learn the Two Triangle Presentation through the following exercise. Find a partner and read through the exercise together.

For our purpose we pick up the counseling in the fourth phase, personal behavior. Jean, the lady we are counseling, has already confessed to being involved with a married man.

THE TWO TRIANGLE PRESENTATION

Counselor: Jean, you're telling me that you are a single Christian woman involved with a married man and that you know this is wrong.

Jean: Yes. I know it's wrong, but I am so confused. I don't know how I feel anymore.

Counselor: I have something I would like to share with you that I believe can help you to better understand your feelings. Here, take this piece of paper and pen. Draw two triangles. (pause) At the top of the first triangle write *Father*. (pause) At the bottom left, write *Son*. (pause) And at the bottom right, write *Holy Spirit* with a capital S.

Jean: (pause) All right.

Counselor: Inside the triangle, write *God*. (pause) God has revealed Himself as Father, Son, and Holy Spirit.

Jean: Okay.

Counselor: Inside the second triangle, write your name. (pause) You and I are made in the image of God. Just as God has revealed Himself in three ways, He has created you and me with three natures. God came to earth in the flesh as Jesus the Christ. He also has given you and me flesh, a body. So at the bottom left of the second triangle write the word *body*. (pause)

Jean: All right.

Counselor: God has also given us a soul. So, at the top of the second triangle write the word *soul*.

(pause) Next to the word *soul,* write *mind and emotions.* (pause) Our soul is where we make our decisions—where we decide to do what we think is right and where we decide to do what we feel we should.

When we pray to God, we are praying to the Master Mind of the universe, the Creator of all things. When we say that God is love, we mean that love is His basic emotion toward us. God has created us like Himself, with the ability to think and feel. We all have a soul and that's where we exercise our free will and make our decisions.

Jean: I see.

Counselor: Now, at the bottom of the triangle on the right-hand side, write the word *spirit* with a small *s.*

Jean: A small *s?*

Counselor: Yes, in the Bible, whenever you see *Spirit* written with a capital *S* that means the "Holy Spirit" of God. And, whenever you see spirit written with a small *s* that means the "spirit" of man.

Jean: Oh!

Counselor: So, here we see: God, the Father; God, the Son; and God, the Holy Spirit as one person. And, we see body; soul; and spirit as one person. (pause) Now, let's look at how we relate to God and how we make our decisions.

At the bottom of your page, write the word *body.* A lot of people allow their body, or their flesh, to control them. If it feels good, they do it. They make decisions based on physical feelings. Their life may be dominated by drugs or alcohol, by sex, or by something else that makes them feel good physically.

You and I know that we must not allow our body to control our lives. We cannot just do whatever might feel good at the moment, can we? That would get us in a lot of trouble.

Jean: That's true.

Counselor: Look back at the bottom of the page. On top of the word body write *emotions*. (pause) Some people allow their feelings to control them. They make emotional decisions. The problem with feelings is that they fluctuate: depending on what someone may have said to us; depending on how much sleep we've had; on how much pizza we ate; depending on any number of things. Our feelings fluctuate! So, decisions based on feelings are inconsistent and unreliable.

Jean: Feelings can be confusing.

Counselor: (pause) That's right. Now, on top of *emotions*, write *mind*. (pause) Here we find the person who says, "I realize I cannot trust my feelings. I am going to think my way through this situation: define the problem, weigh the alternatives, make a decision, and take action." The problem is, when we lean on our own understanding, we may not have all the facts. Even when we have all the information, we can still be confused.

A glass may be half full or half empty. It's

a matter of perception. So, we can't always depend on our knowledge and our understanding. There are times when we have all the facts, yet we are still confused. Isn't that right?

Jean: Yes, that's true.

Counselor: So we can't always trust our mind to guide us either. There may be times when physically, we 'feel' like doing one thing. Emotionally, we may not be sure how we 'feel.' Mentally, we may 'know' that we should not do something. So, a battle takes place within us.

By the way, draw a bracket around mind and emotion and write the word *soul*. This is to remind us that our soul (ME) contains our mind and emotions.

Now, go up the page about four spaces and write *Father*. (pause)

Here we are body and soul cut off from our Heavenly Father. Our sin separates us from our Heavenly Father. The penalty for sin is death. But God loves us so much that He came in the person of Jesus Christ and died in payment for our sins. Under Father write *Jesus*.

Jean: Okay.

Counselor: The moment we accept Jesus Christ as our Savior three wonderful things happen to us. First, our sins are forgiven. Second, we receive the gift of eternal life. And third, God's Holy Spirit comes to live inside of us.

In your diagram, under Jesus, write *Holy Spirit* with a capital S. (pause)

When the Holy Spirit comes to live inside of us we are 'born again.' Under *Holy Spirit* write *spirit* with a small *s*. (pause)

Jean, you told me earlier you had accepted Jesus as your Savior, so this symbolizes your spirit, born in Christ, to live forever. Draw a circle around *Holy Spirit* and *spirit*. (pause)

Jean: Okay.

Counselor: The circle symbolizes that God's Holy Spirit comes to live in us forever, that we are in Him and He is in us.

Jean, here we see the Trinity of God—Father, Son, and Holy Spirit—united with the trinity of man—body, soul, and spirit. According to 1 John 4:4, the wonderful message is that "the one who is in you is greater than the one who is in the world" (NIV). God is greater and more powerful than Satan or the temptation and sin of this world.

Let me share something else with you. Open your Bible and read 1 Corinthians 10:13 (NIV).

Jean: "No temptation has seized you except what is common to man. And God is faithful; he will not let you be tempted beyond what you can bear. But when you are tempted, he will also provide a way out so that you can stand up under it."

Counselor: Jean, as a Christian, you have the power of God within you to resist the relationship with the married man.

But, let's go back to the beginning. How did you first meet Jack?

Jean: We met at the apartment complex swimming pool. He is very good looking and has a lot of personality. He just, you know, came over to where I was at the pool and started talking to me. He wasn't wearing a ring. I didn't know he was married. (pause)

Our relationship took off like a rocket. It didn't slow down until two weeks ago. He was and is just the most wonderful person I've ever dated. The only problem is that he is married. I felt guilty about what happened, but no one else seemed to notice. You would not believe how much sleeping around goes on in our apartment complex.

Jack is the best looking man I have ever dated. I should have been wary when things were happening so fast, but it just felt so good. It was so exciting, and romantic! (pause) He was so attentive and caring. We were together all the time! He paid so much attention to me. It's like he didn't even see the other girls.

Then, he disappeared for two weeks. I later found out that he had bought a house and was off moving his wife and family. He called me once and told me he was out of town. Later, I saw the Resident Manager showing his apartment. When he called the next time I confronted him and that's when he told me that he was moving his wife and family into a house that he had bought. He said it like he assumed that I knew he was married, but he never told me.

Then he said that . . . that he loved me. I cried all week.

He called yesterday and said that he is

coming over tomorrow, Saturday afternoon. I don't know what to do. I want to see him. I really do, but, I know it's wrong.

Counselor: (pause) You know it's wrong. (pause) What do you mean by that?

Jean: You know, that he's married; that we're not, you know.

Counselor: Yes, I know. (pause) What do you think about sex outside of marriage?
[Note: think not feel]

Jean: It's wrong. I have always known that.

Counselor: Is Jack the first man that you have been to bed with?

Jean: No, there was a boy in college. I . . . I thought that we would get married too, but it didn't work out that way.

Counselor: It seems like you are still a little in shock. You don't know quite how you feel, what to do. Part of you wants to be with him again and part of you knows that it would never work out. He is married, and you know that the relationship is wrong.

Jean: That's about it. (pause) He mentioned his wife to me like somebody would talk about his car or boat. He's married but he doesn't feel like that should affect our relationship. (pause)

He seems so warm and loving when he is with me, but he talks about his wife like . . . I don't know.

Counselor: He is very warm and loving when he is with you and he wants to be romantic and have sex, but he did deceive you. He didn't tell you that he is married. (pause)

He acts as though his commitment to his wife and children means nothing to him, and expects that you should not let his wife and family stand in the way of your being together.

Jean: (Silent)

Counselor: Jean, look back at the paper you were writing on. (pause) You see how we have a body, a soul, and a spirit?

Jean: Yes.

Counselor: Our sinful flesh draws us to physical pleasure and can pull us in the wrong direction, if we are not careful.

Jean: But it was not like that!

Counselor: I see. (pause) You know, while men are often motivated physically, women are more often motivated emotionally. Our emotions are feelings as well, and feelings can get us into trouble. Mentally, we know that we should not do something, but we emotionally allow strong feelings to pull us the wrong way.

We may be lonely. (pause) We may need love. (pause) We may meet someone who is very attractive. We are drawn to them. They respond. It happens so fast.

An affair with a married man is like that. It can be exciting, but it's like a roller coaster. It takes you up and down, round and round— but it leaves you nowhere. (pause)

	Spiritually, you have already told me that it is a sin for you to be with Jack.
Jean:	Is it a sin just to be with him? I mean, if we don't have sex?
Counselor:	Would you be stealing moments with him that he should be spending with his wife?
Jean:	He said he loves me!
Counselor:	Is he married? (pause) Is it not reasonable to assume, given the relationship you have had, that if you continue to see him that you would end up back in bed with him? (pause) Is this a relationship that you can be proud of or is this a relationship that you have to hide? (pause) What would Jesus say?
Jean:	(long pause) Okay, but how do I change the way I feel?
Counselor:	God will help you to change your feelings and to put this situation behind you, but first, let me ask you a question. Tell me, what is the difference between *confession* and *repentance?*
Jean:	Confession and repentance? I guess confession is where you acknowledge that something is wrong, and repentance is where you ask forgiveness and promise not to do it again.
Counselor:	Very good! Jean, you have confessed to me that your relationship with Jack is wrong. God knows all about it. He knows your heart and He understands how lonely you have been. He knows all the details of your sin, and He still loves you.
When we sin, He asks us to come to Him

and acknowledge the sins we have committed. If we belong to Christ, and you do, He tells us in advance that He will forgive us, but He wants us to come to Him with a repentant heart. He promises to give us the strength not to sin again if we will turn to Him.

Jean, would you like to pray together with me right now and ask God to forgive you for this sin?

Jean: Yes, I would.

Counselor: Okay, you pray aloud first, and then I will pray with you. Tell God that you are sorry, ask Him to forgive you through the blood of Jesus Christ, and tell Him that you will not do this again.

Jean: Do I have to pray aloud?

Counselor: Sure! That's the only way I can hear what you say and know what I should pray. Just talk to Him like you have been talking with me, then I will join you in prayer.

Here, let me help you get started: Heavenly Father, we thank You that we can come to You at any hour of the day or night, that You are always waiting to talk with us, that You love us, that You will forgive us for our sins if we will come to You in the name of Jesus Christ with a repentant heart. Thank You for bringing Jean and me together. Guide her now, oh God. As she comes to You, give her the words to say. In Jesus' name, I pray.

Jean: (pause, soft crying) Oh God . . . please forgive me! I know it was wrong for me to sleep with

Jack. I knew it was wrong even before I knew he was married. I promise not to see him again. I promise not to have sex with anybody again, until I'm married. (crying) If I get married. (pause) Oh God! (crying) Help me to keep this prayer. In Jesus' name.

Counselor: (pause) Heavenly Father, thank You for Your forgiveness! Thank You for revealing the truth to Jean and for calling her to confess her sin to You. Thank You, oh God, that she has now been forgiven. Fill her with Your Holy Spirit we pray. Give her the Power and the strength to turn away from temptation. Give her Your Peace, Your Power, and Your Protection, we pray in the name of Jesus. Amen! (Silent)

Jean: (pause) Thank you.

Counselor: Now, write this down, and we will talk about it later: *Love is not a feeling. Love is a commitment.*

Jean: Love is not a feeling?

Counselor: That's right. *Love is not a feeling. Love is a commitment.* (pause) Got it?

Jean: Yes.

Counselor: Okay, we will come back and talk about that in a minute. First, let's go back to your paper where you wrote body, soul, and spirit.

Jean: Okay.

Counselor: Jean, the Greek language, in which the New Testament was written, has three words for love: *eros, philos,* and *agape.* The English language translates these three words into one word *love*.

We know that when a person says, 'I love your house,' the meaning is quite different from when a person holds you in his arms and says, 'I love you,' isn't it?

Jean: Yes, I should hope so.

Counselor: Well, I'd like to talk about those three Greek words that we translate into the English word *love*.

On your paper next to the word body write the word *eros*.

You are familiar with the word erotic, a sexual, sensual kind of love. Eros is also a selfish, conditional, demanding kind of love. "I love you, as long as you give me what I want." "I love you as long as you give me: sex, social position, or security," for example. Eros is not very satisfying. A person eventually feels used. Eros is a 'conditional' love; I love you if you give me what I want.

Skip up a line, and next to the word soul write *philos*.

Philos is the root word from which we get Philadelphia, the city of brotherly love. Philos is a mutual love. I'll scratch your back, if you scratch mine. "I give to you as you give to me, true love," the song says. Emotionally, philos is more satisfying than eros. Both people are giving. Intellectually, it seems more fair. I'll give to you what you give to me. But let's take a closer look.

"You hug me, and I'll hug you back." That gets a desired result. "You hurt me, and I'll hurt you." That doesn't take us where we want to go. "You hit me, and I'll hit you back." Now, we are really going in the wrong direction.

On your paper next to spirit, write *agape.* Tell me what you know about agape love.

Jean: Not very much. Isn't agape like God's love?

Counselor: Yes, let's look at God's love.

God loves us even when we hurt Him, even when we disobey Him. Agape is the kind of love that continues for richer or for poorer in sickness and in health. Agape is the kind of love that is based on *commitment,* not on *feeling.* Jack could give you eros as long as you gave him what he wanted. He could give you philos as long as the two of you made each other feel good. Jack could not give you agape love because he could not make a *commitment* to you.

Love is not a feeling. Love is a commitment.

Jean: I understand, that really helps, but how do I change the way I feel?

Counselor: I am glad you asked. Take a look at your paper again. Do you see how *mind* is on top of *emotions* which is on top of *body?* Next to the word *mind* write *thoughts.*

Next to the word *emotions* write *feelings.* Next to the word *body* write *actions.*

Jean: Okay.

Counselor: Proverbs 23:7 says, "For as he thinks in his heart, so is he." In other words: Controlling your thoughts is the answer to controlling your feelings and ultimately to controlling your behavior.

If you were to start telling me about one of the funniest things that ever happened to you, about a time when you were with some people that you really enjoyed being with, you would start to smile, you would begin to feel good, your body chemistry would actually change. On the other hand, if you were to tell me about a very sad time in your life, your face would change, you would begin to feel depressed and heavy, your body chemistry would change.

Jean: That's true!

Counselor: Your thoughts control your feelings and ultimately how you behave. You have simply got to put this sinful relationship behind you. Do not see him again. God has forgiven you. Forgive yourself. Refuse to think about it. God will help you to control your thoughts, and your feelings.

Jean: Okay!

Counselor: Write down this number: 933-3991.

Jean: What's that?

Counselor: This is the telephone number of SINGLE AGAPE. That's a Christian Singles Group. They meet on Friday nights. Call that number and ask to speak to Molly. She will arrange for a single woman your age to call on you and perhaps meet you for lunch before the next meeting. SINGLE AGAPE has a lot of differ-

	ent activities. I think you will enjoy the group, perhaps make some new friends.
Jean:	O.K., I'll give them a try. Thank you for your help!
Counselor:	I'm glad I was here.
Jean:	Me too.
Counselor:	Call us again?
Jean:	I will. You have helped me so much! Thank you.
Counselor:	Good night!
Jean:	Good night!

The Two Triangle presentation can be used anywhere. You can draw it on a paper napkin while counseling with a friend in a restaurant or on a plane. You can also have them draw it as you talk over the phone. The drawings structure the ideas being presented and help the person to see what is being said.

There are actually three presentations. First, there is the basic Two Triangle presentation that helps the person to better understand God, himself, and his relationship to God. The triangles and the column help a person to see the Gospel and the relationship we have with the Holy Spirit. The second presentation helps a person to better understand the different types of love, and his love relationships. It helps the person to better understand the behavior of others who may have hurt him. The third presentation helps a person to better understand how thoughts control desires and, ultimately, behavior. It illustrates how our spirit is alive in His Spirit and that we should let the mind that is in Christ Jesus dwell in us and resist sinful thoughts.

Learn how to present all three aspects of the Two Triangle presentation. This is easy for the person to follow and understand!

CLOSING DEVOTION
Personal Character

READER ONE: A person's character reflects who he is when no one else is around. A Christian businessman is out of town on a trip. In his motel room, pay television is offering programs depicting nudity and sexual situations. He could watch the programs in the seclusion of his room. No one would ever know—except God. His character will determine how he deals with the temptation. His character will grow stronger or weaker by his decision.

READER TWO: A young boy needs to make a good grade on the final exam if he is to pass the course. The girl sitting next to him is a good student. She is not careful about covering her paper. Will the young boy look on her paper and compare answers? It is a matter of character.

READER ONE: Each time we turn away a particular temptation, our character grows stronger and we have more control over that particular temptation. Each time we yield to a temptation, we become weaker in character and that temptation has a stronger appeal and more control over us.

READER TWO: A man was trying to stop smoking. He would throw away his cigarettes, vow to stop smoking, and succeed in his effort for weeks and sometimes even months at a time. Then, the time would come when he would be with some friends. The smell of the cigarette smoke would be so appealing. His buddy across the table, forgetting that he has stopped smoking, offers him a cigarette. It is a matter of character. Will he say, "Oh well, just one," and fall again?

READER ONE: Every day we all face temptations. As we turn away from these temptations, our character grows stronger and the hold and the appeal of those temptations grow weaker. God gives us the ability to say No, the free will to make decisions from which our character will grow stronger or become weaker.

READER TWO: Hear what the Word of God says in First Corinthians 10:13: "No temptation has overtaken you except such as is common to man; but God is faithful, who will not allow you to be tempted beyond what you are able, but with the temptation will also make the way of escape, that you may be able to bear it."

READER ONE: God is at work in us to help build our Christian character. He will protect us. We read wonderful news in First John 4:4, "He who is in you is greater than he who is in the world." God will not allow Satan to overpower us.

READER TWO: At the same time, we must remember the prayer of Jesus from Matthew 6:13, "And do not lead us into temptation, / But deliver us from the evil one." We must be careful not to entertain or play around with the temptation. As James 4:7 says, "Therefore submit to God. Resist the devil and he will flee from you."

READER ONE: Life is a series of small choices. Jesus said in Luke 16:10, "He who is faithful in what is least is faithful also in much." As we become faithful and obedient in the decisions pertaining to our own life, God will be able to use us to reach others.

READER TWO: As we privately worship God each day and ask His Holy Spirit to fill us and transform us through the renewing of our mind, as we fill our mind with Scripture, and spend time each day in prayer, we will grow strong in Christ Jesus. As we live out an obedient life, God will use us to reach our family, our neighbor, and our friends for Him.

READER ONE: We are His modern-day disciples. There is so much God wants to do through us. May all that we think and do be pleasing in His sight as we minister together in Christ Jesus.

READER TWO: (Closing Prayer)

Chapter 11

Know What You Believe

In Colossians we are warned about the false teaching of the world. "Beware lest anyone cheat you through philosophy and empty deceit, . . . according to the basic principles of the world, and not according to Christ. For in Him dwells all the fullness of the Godhead bodily; and you are complete in Him, who is the head of all principality and power" (2:8–10).

All of us know friends and family members who go to different churches, who perhaps have vastly different political views, who may or may not spend much time at home or church studying the Bible. While denominations differ on how communion is served, how the church addresses social and political issues, or how much water is needed for baptism, certain "bedrock beliefs" have united Christians for centuries. For nearly two thousand years, the followers of Christ have affirmed certain basic tenets of the Christian faith.

For Christians counseling with individuals in crisis or recovery knowing these foundational beliefs is essential in guiding someone through confusing questions of faith, doctrine, and personal salvation. As we seek to help people who are reaching out in a time of crisis, we must realize that they may come from a Christian background different from our own. They may have grown up with negative feelings about the church. Yet, during times of crisis, people are often much more open to the saving message of the Gospel. Opportunities for sharing your faith may present themselves. Therefore, it is beneficial to review these "bedrock beliefs." Having a good understanding of basic Christian beliefs equips you to respond more wisely, compassionately, and responsibly to someone who is seeking a greater meaning in life and longing for a closer relationship with God.

After reviewing the basic tenets of the Christian faith, we will look at the issue of the authority of the Bible, and then review counseling guidelines for working with non-Christians.

JESUS CHRIST, OUR GOD AND SAVIOR

The cornerstone of Christianity is Jesus Christ Himself. Other religions, such as Buddhism and Islam, evolved from a "prophet" or a gifted teacher. But Christianity is unique in a very significant way: Only the Christian tradition offers an *incarnational* faith. God became man through the historic person of Jesus Christ as a way of reaching out to a fallen world and reconciling us to Him. The most famous verse in the Bible says, "For God so loved the world that He gave His only begotten Son, that whoever believes in Him should not perish but have everlasting life" (John 3:16).

Jesus identified Himself as God, and His actions as recorded in the New Testament proved that He was fully human and fully divine. Christians believe that Jesus was not merely a prophet through whom the power of God flowed, nor simply the Son of God; rather, the Bible is clear that Jesus and the Father are one. (See John 14.)

A discussion of these spiritual beliefs might be confusing to a person in crisis who may feel that his life has come unraveled. Also, the Bible says that only a spiritual man can discern spiritual things (1 Cor. 2:11–16). That is why spiritual growth and understanding really take place in phases four and five of the counseling model, after comforting the person (phase one), offering counsel about the problem (phase two), and bringing the one in crisis to a personal relationship with Christ (phase three). Then, with the Holy Spirit in him, the person can begin to understand the Bible and what it means to be a Christian.

Now, it is time to ask the questions, Who is the man they call Jesus? And, Is Jesus God?

Let's take a close look at what Jesus said and did.

1. Jesus forgave sins, allowed the disciples to worship Him, and claimed to have all authority over heaven and earth. Only God can forgive sins. Only God is to be worshiped. Only God has all power and authority.

Mark 2:5	When Jesus saw their faith, He said to the paralytic, "Son, your sins are forgiven you."
Matthew 14:33	Then those who were in the boat came and worshiped Him, saying, "Truly You are the Son of God."
John 20:28	And Thomas answered and said unto Him, "My Lord and my God!"
Matthew 28:18	And Jesus came and spoke to them, saying, "All authority has been given to Me in heaven and on earth."

2. Jesus revealed that He existed before the beginning of time, that He was with the Father before creation, and claimed to be alive at the time of Abraham.

John 17:5	"And now, O Father, glorify Me together with Yourself, with the glory

which I had with You before the world was."

John 8:58   Jesus said to them, "Most assuredly, I say to you, before Abraham was, I AM."

3. Finally, one of the disciples who was with Jesus day after day during His three years of ministry on earth wrote that Jesus was God in the flesh. The Gospel of John begins with these beautiful words:

John 1:1, 14   "In the beginning was the Word, and the Word was with God, and the Word was God. . . . And the Word became flesh and dwelt among us."

A well-known Christian apologist once said, "Either Jesus Christ is who He claimed to be (God) or He was a liar. There is no in-between." Yet one cannot read the New Testament without also encountering references to God the Father and God the Holy Spirit. The Father, Jesus, and the Holy Spirit make up the personage of the Trinity. Christians of every denomination and every generation have written countless books about the Trinity. Why? Because the Trinity is one of those "bedrock beliefs" that bind Christians together and that's what we'll turn our attention to next.

THE TRIUNE GOD

Christians believe that there is only one God and He is the source of all creation. The concept of the Trinity does not compromise this basic belief.

God revealed Himself to us first as God the Father. As we have already discussed, God, the Father, sent God, the Son, into the world as the Redeemer. John 3:17 says, "For God did not send His Son into the world to condemn the world, but that the world through Him might be saved." At the Last Supper Jesus promised that the Holy Spirit would be sent to us and that He would always be with us.

"And I will pray the Father, and He will give you another Helper, that He may abide with you forever. . . . But the Helper, the Holy Spirit, whom the Father will send in My name, He will teach you all things, and bring to your remembrance all things that I said to you" (John 14:16, 26).

We must remember that God created time and space. He is able to be in all places at all times. We, on the other hand, are finite and can only be in one place at a time. God is able to go to the Methodist church, the Baptist church, and the Presbyterian church—all at the same time. He is able to be in Rome, Georgia and Rome, Italy, at the same time. He is able to be in heaven and earth at the same time.

An analogy that may bring greater clarity to the concept of the Trinity is found in a cup of water. Water can take the form of a life-giving liquid or it can be a rock-solid, tangible substance when frozen. When heat is applied, water becomes a vapor, steam. If water can change its form from liquid to solid to vapor, certainly God, who created the water, has no problem revealing Himself in different forms while remaining the same. In each form, liquid, vapor, or solid, water meets different needs. So it is with God.

For a review of the characteristics of the Trinity, let's go to the Scriptures.

The Characteristics of God, the Father

- The Heavenly Father   1 Peter 1:2

- The source of all life   Genesis 1:1;
                                       Colossians 1:16–17

• Eternal creator of time and space	Revelation 1:8; Psalm 139:7
• A personal being who loves, hates, grieves, and cares	John 3:16; Proverbs 6:16; Genesis 6:6; 1 Peter 5:7

The Characteristics of God, the Son

• God Incarnate: God coming into the world as a human, born of a virgin	Matthew 1:23
• Died upon the cross in payment for our sins	2 Corinthians 5:21; John 3:17
• Suffered, died, and rose again	1 Peter 3:18; Luke 24:46–49
• The redeemer who reconciles us	John 14:2–3, 6

The Characteristics of God, the Holy Spirit

• The Spirit of God who lives within us once we accept Jesus Christ as our Savior	John 3:3–6; John 14:16
• Our teacher and guide	John 16:13
• Convicts us of our sin	John 16:8–9
• Reveals the truth to us	John 16:13
• Gives us faith	1 Corinthians 12:9
• Lives within us	1 Corinthians 6:19
• Seals us in faith and fills us with the Spirit of the living Christ	Ephesians 1:13; 5:18
• Empowers us	Acts 1:8

As Christians we have been created by the Father, redeemed by the Son, and empowered by the Holy Spirit. Although we live in a sinful, broken world, we can have victory over whatever trials, temptations, or difficult circumstances we may face. This is the hope we have to offer to those we counsel.

A FALLEN WORLD

We have used words such as *redeemed* and *reconciled*. Yet one may wonder, "Redeemed from what?" or "Reconciled to what?" Why is redemption or reconciliation necessary? To answer these questions, we have to look briefly at the concept of sin, a concept long disdained in our society.

Living a life of moral integrity has never been easy. Our contemporary culture is, in many ways, at odds with the values we are called to as Christians. Secular psychology has permeated the media, the entertainment industry, public schools, and public figures, even family and friends who express popularly accepted truisms with which we are all familiar:

- If it feels good, do it.
- Feelings are neither good nor bad; they just are.
- All things are acceptable if done in moderation.
- We are products of heredity and environment, and are therefore not responsible for who we are or what we do.
- Anything that two consenting adults want to do should be permitted, as long as nobody else gets hurt.
- Morality cannot be legislated.
- Nobody has the right to tell me what to do.
- Sin is an old-fashioned, outdated word that doesn't mean anything anymore.
- What's wrong for you, may be right for me.

We've heard these messages so often that they begin to sound acceptable but they contradict the teachings of the Bible. Theologians point out that this humanistic philosophy is based on "situational ethics." Situational ethics basically means that what is wrong in one situation may be right or acceptable in another and the underlying philosophy is an absence of absolutes, an absence of clearly defined right and wrong. Yet, this absence of absolutes conflicts with the teachings of the Bible. God makes it clear. There really is right and wrong. There really is sin.

SIN AND TEMPTATION

The Christian faith embraces the concept of sin, recognizing that "all have sinned and fall short of the glory of God" (Rom. 3:23). Sin separates us from God. Before accepting Jesus Christ, we may be completely unaware of our sinful nature. Denial is not a new discovery of the modern age!

The apostle Paul was well aware of our human tendency toward spiritual blindness when he wrote these words in one of the earliest letters of the New Testament to the church at Corinth: "But the natural man does not receive the things of the Spirit of God, for they are foolishness to him; nor can he know them, because they are spiritually discerned" (1 Cor. 2:14). And several decades later, John also spoke to the issue of our blindness to sin: "If we say that we have no sin, we deceive ourselves, and the truth is not in us. If we confess our sins, He is faithful and just to forgive us our sins and to cleanse us from all unrighteousness" (1 John 1:8–9).

God works in our hearts through the power of the Holy Spirit to convict us of our sin, and in so doing enables us to see our need for Christ. Yet even after we commit our lives to Christ, we are continually confronted with temptation. Each of us face difficult choices, compromising situations, or tempting opportunities, and know within ourselves that what we are facing would not be pleasing to God. There will be times of temptation for every Christian, times we will have to turn away from something that would bring pleasure or something that "everybody else" seems to be doing. As Christians we are not exempt from pain, heartache, rejection, and loneliness. Doing what is right and resisting temptation are seldom easy.

In the short run it may seem difficult for a person who is hurting to refuse pleasure, or for the lonely person to walk away from friends engaged in sinful activities. After all, sex *feels good*. Drugs *feel good*. Stealing, cheating, and getting even are exciting and *feel good*. Sin offers a *sin*sation, but like a roller coaster ride, the gratification is short-lived and the ride takes us nowhere.

We each have a choice. We can grab for instant gratification or "wait upon the Lord" for the real thing. God gives His children the ability to say no! We have only to look to Christ for the strength to withstand temptations.

However, let's be clear on the difference between sin and temptation. Temptation itself is not sin. Even Jesus was tempted—but did not sin. In the temptation story found in Matthew 4:1–11, Jesus called upon His knowledge of the Scripture, and He turned away from the tempting situation. Later, He taught His disciples to pray, "Lead us not into temptation, but deliver us from evil" (Matt. 6:13 KJV).

As Christians we can arm ourselves against the temptation of sin through the faithfulness of God with Scripture: "No temptation has overtaken you except such as is common to man; but God is faithful, who will not allow you to be tempted beyond what you are able, but with the temptation will also make the way of escape, that you may be able to bear it" (1 Cor. 10:13).

The keys to turning away from temptation are:

- Studying God's Word.
- Making a commitment to live in a manner pleasing to God.
- Calling upon the Holy Spirit for help.
- Resisting temptation in the name of Jesus Christ.
- Removing oneself from tempting situations.
- Learning to control one's thoughts.

NEW LIFE IN CHRIST

Paul, writing to the church in Corinth said, "Therefore, if anyone is *in Christ,* he is a new creation; old things have passed away; behold, all things have become new" (2 Cor. 5:17, emphasis added).

When we accepted Jesus Christ as our Savior, we received the Holy Spirit of God (John 14:16), and with Him, we have the ability to turn away from sin. The same Spirit of God who created and rules the universe is alive in us, and there is no limit to what God can do when we turn to Him.

We may be weak, but He is strong. Alcohol, drugs? There is no habit that is too strong for God to overcome. Hatred, anger, fear, depression? There is no emotion, no mental or physical or behavioral problem that God cannot heal. Christ has redeemed us from the bondage of sin. We are free to do God's will (Rom. 6:18).

If we will give the Holy Spirit control of our lives, He will transform us, heal us, restore us, and give us love, joy, peace, and self-control—the abundant life (Gal. 5:22).

LIFE ETERNAL

Jesus said, "I am the resurrection and the life. He who believes in Me, though he may die, he shall live. And whoever lives and believes in Me shall never die" (John 11:25–26).

The most wonderful, priceless gift is given to us when we accept Jesus Christ as Savior and Lord. It is the gift of eternal life. We have the promise and assurance from God that we will live with Him forever.

We are born into this world with a physical body which eventually ends in physical death. But through the death and resurrection of Jesus Christ, we who believe can *know* that our physical death is merely a passage into eternal life, united with God forever. We *know* this to be true because Jesus rose from the dead. Our belief is in our redemption (Rom. 8:23), unto eternal life (1 John 5:13), through the sacrifice Jesus made for us (Heb. 8 and 9).

"Thanks be to God for His indescribable gift!" (2 Cor. 9:15).

A LIFE TO COME

Many people no longer believe that a literal heaven or hell exist. To consider the reality of heaven and hell implies the certainty of judgment, something many people do not *want* to believe. The Old and New Testaments, however, have numerous references to a final judgment day, to heaven and to hell.

Jesus told His disciples when the Son of Man (Christ) sits on His throne of glory and the nations are brought before Him, people who failed to follow the path of righteousness will be told, "'Depart from Me, you cursed, into the everlasting fire prepared for the devil and his angels.' . . . And these will go away into everlasting punishment, but the righteous into eternal life" (Matt. 25:41, 46).

Christians have the assurance of eternal life. Through the resurrection, Christ overcame death and His blood upon the mercy seat paid for our sins (see Heb. 8 and 9). At the Last Supper, Jesus told His disciples, "In My Father's house are many mansions; if it were not so, I would have told you. I go to prepare a place for you. And if I go and prepare a place for you, I will come again and receive you to Myself; that where I am, there you may be also" (John 14:2–3).

The disciples could not fully comprehend the words of Jesus that night. Much later, after witnessing the events of the crucifixion of Jesus, His death, and resurrection, only then did the full meaning of His words at the Last Supper become clear. Years later, John wrote in his first letter to the early church, "These things I have written to you who believe in the name of the Son of God, that you may know that you have eternal life" (1 John 5:13).

THE WORD OF GOD

We have covered the basic beliefs of Christianity:

- Jesus Christ, our God and Savior
- The Triune God
- A Fallen World and Temptation
- New Life in Christ
- A New Creation
- Life Eternal

As we have addressed each of these doctrines, we have returned again and again to the Bible as our basis for these beliefs. Why? What's so special about a book, written by some thirty-five men over a period of about fifteen hundred years? The Holy Bible, a collection of sixty-six separate books, was written by men who came from vastly differing cultures, separated by centuries; men who spoke different languages and came from a wide variety of family and educational backgrounds. Some were educated; some were not. Some were kings, some were fishermen. Yet, for all the many differences in culture, language, and time, the writers of the sixty-six books in the Holy Bible share one thing in common: they were inspired by God.

The very fact that these separate books come together as one book, a book which has survived centuries of changing governments, war, natural and man-made disasters, language differences, and cultural barriers is a miracle only God could have brought about.

The inspiration and authority of Scripture is remarkable. But to understand why, one has to know a little about the history of the Scriptures as we now know them. Scripture began with what scholars call "oral and written traditions," that is, the telling and retelling of the teachings of God. Eventually, the early Christian church identified which books and writings were authoritative in what is called the canon, the academic term for the collection of sacred writings. Later, biblical writers began the process of meticulously writing and copying those teachings. In the centuries before printing presses, multiple copies of the sacred writings could be created only by men called scribes, who dedicated their lives to the task of copying and re-copying the sacred texts.

The Christian church has *always* affirmed that the living presence of the Holy Spirit guided and illumined the entire process of canonization (or collection) of the sixty-six books of the Bible, from the oral and written traditions to the contemporary translations we now hold before us as we study God's inspired Word.

Archaeologists made an exciting discovery in 1947 that underscores the divine nature of this process and the miraculous accuracy of the text.

While climbing among the cliffs of Qumran near the Dead Sea, a young shepherd began throwing stones into the caves at the top of the cliffs. Hearing what sounded like breaking glass, the boy explored further, finding dusty clay pots filled with scrolls. Not knowing what he had discovered, but assuming these clay pots were worth *something,* he took a scrap of the scrolls into the nearest town. When the scrolls were placed in the hands of a trained biblical archaeologist, the discovery was heralded as the greatest archaeological find of the century.

Now called the Dead Sea Scrolls, these ancient documents pre-date any other early manuscripts by at least one thousand years. The clay pots, hidden away in the caves of Qumran for nearly two thousand years, contained fragments from every book of the Old Testament with the exception of the book of Esther. The Dead Sea Scrolls contained *complete* manuscripts of Deuteronomy, Isaiah, Psalms, and several other books.

When scholars studied these ancient documents and compared them to modern Scripture, their findings confirmed the accuracy of the texts. What does that mean? Remarkably, discovery after discovery confirms that the Word of God has been accurately preserved.

Jesus Himself accepted the authority of Scripture, saying in the Sermon on the Mount, "For assuredly, I say to you, till heaven and earth pass away, one jot or one tittle will by no means pass from the law till all is fulfilled" (Matt. 5:18). A jot or tittle is a minute part. Here Jesus is saying that not even a minute part of Scripture will be changed—that God will preserve His Word through the centuries. And He has!

The ultimate proof of the divine nature of the Holy Bible is the wisdom found within its pages and the transformed lives of the people who follow its teachings. New discoveries, advanced technologies, and contemporary research limit the lifespan and usefulness of many books published only a few years ago, rendering inaccurate and out-of-date what was once considered cutting-edge. Yet, the Bible is as fresh as tomorrow's newspaper with wisdom and direction for people of every culture, every century, and every circumstance.

Christians can trust in the Bible as God's Word, a source of guidance, comfort, conviction, and wisdom—the ultimate guide for how we live our lives.

WHAT YOU NEED TO KNOW

In working with individuals in crisis, we have already addressed the priority of caring for their immediate needs before trying to address their spiritual condition. As you see an individual through a crisis, the Holy Spirit may provide an opportunity for you to share your faith with that person. You may feel anxious, concerned that you may "say the wrong thing" or "turn the person off from God."

Don't dismay. Even Moses was nervous when faced with the prospect of speaking out for the Lord! In Exodus 4:10 Moses tells God that he doesn't think quickly on his feet and can't speak eloquently. But God reassures Moses by saying, "Who has made man's mouth? Or who makes the mute, the deaf, the seeing, or the blind? Have not I, the LORD? Now therefore, go, and I will be with your mouth and teach you what you shall say" (Ex. 4:11). Trust in the assurance that if you have an opportunity to share your faith, you are not alone. The Holy Spirit is with you and will guide you.

You have studied the bedrock beliefs of Christianity. You have prepared yourself for an opportunity such as this. Your job is to be faithful; the Holy Spirit's job is to convict a person of his sin, reveal the truth of Jesus Christ, and give the person the faith to believe. To be most effective in relating with the person, especially the non-Christian, consider the following guidelines:

1. *Never argue* with a person regarding their beliefs or yours. Whether the issue that arises is the authority of the Bible, questions about the existence of heaven or hell, or even the deity of Christ, arguing about one's beliefs is rarely productive.

2. Instead, *listen and ask questions.* Let the other person talk about their questions or beliefs.

3. After listening to the other person, *ask if he or she is willing to listen to another viewpoint.* Then, share your testimony, talking personally about the difference Christ has made in your life. A person cannot argue with your experience.

4. *Present the Home Run Presentation of the Gospel.* Until the person is saved and has the Holy Spirit living inside him, he cannot understand the deeper things of God. Only the spiritual man can discern spiritual things.

5. You may also want to
   - Give the person a modern translation of the Bible and suggest passages to read.
   - Invite the person to a church that offers biblically based teaching.
   - Offer to meet regularly with the person for Bible study, to listen, counsel, and pray with him or her.

- Continue to invite the person to receive Jesus Christ as his Lord and Savior.

When you confront sinful or destructive behavior, *don't tell the person what he or she "should" or "should not" be doing.* This type of direct confrontation will only make the person feel condemned or judged, resulting in a breakdown of the relationship. Instead, ask the person what he or she *thinks* about the behavior. Use the word *think,* not *feel.* Sinful behavior may *feel* good, yet the person knows what he or she is doing is wrong. For example:

"Tom, what do you think about living with Mary and not being married?"

6. If a person is committed to a sinful life-style, you may not be able to change his or her perspective or behavior. You can continue to love and accept the person, even though his or her behavior is unacceptable. Until the person is ready to repent, confesses his or her sinfulness, and receive Jesus Christ as his or her personal Savior, attitudes, behavior, and life-style cannot be truly changed. Only through the power of the Holy Spirit can a person be transformed.

Although the most important thing in life is to repent of our sins and commit our lives to Christ, one person cannot force another to believe or change. Even God will not overpower a person. What you can do for friends or family members who have not accepted Christ as their Lord and Savior is really quite simple: You can love them and pray for them. Prior to presenting the Gospel to someone, pray that God will:

- Convict the person of his or her sins (John 16:8).
- Reveal the truth of Jesus Christ (John 14:26).
- Give the person the faith to believe (Eph. 2:8).

HOMEWORK
Chapter 11

Name _____

Date _____

Group Leader _____

Hand in to Group Leader during your next class.

Memorize the following Scripture verses.

1. Write out John 14:16.

   "And I will pray the Father, and He will _____

   _____

   _____

   _____

   _____

   _____."

2. Write out John 14:26.

   "But the Helper, the Holy Spirit, whom the Father will send
   in My name, _____

   _____

   _____

   _____

   _____

   _____."

3. Write out Galatians 5:22.

   "But the fruit of the Spirit is _____

   _____

   _____

_____

_____

_____."

4. Write out 1 Corinthians 10:13.

"No temptation has overtaken you except such as is common to man; but God is faithful, _____

_____

_____

_____

_____."

5. Write out Romans 12:2.

"Do not be conformed to this world, but _____

_____

_____

_____

_____."

Doctrinal Review

Place the letter or letters that you believe to be true in the space provided. *There may be more than one answer.*

___ 6. The Bible . . .

(A) was written by man, translated several times, contains basic truth, but is not to be taken literally.

(B) is comprised of sixty-six books written over some fifteen hundred years and contradicts itself in several places.

(C) was written by men under the inspiration of the Holy Spirit. It is God's Holy Word and can be relied on completely.

___ 7. Sin . . .

    (A) is relative. For example, a man who steals bread to feed his starving child is not committing a sin.

    (B) is clearly identified in the Bible.

    (C) has been committed by everyone.

___ 8. Temptation . . .

    (A) is not a sin, unless one begins to fantasize upon forbidden behavior.

    (B) is not a sin, and fantasizing about forbidden behavior is not a sin either. A person only sins if he or she actually carries out the act.

    (C) should be avoided.

___ 9. God . . .

    (A) is our heavenly Father. Jesus is His Son. Jesus is not God.

    (B) has revealed Himself to man as: God, the Father; God, the Son; and God, the Holy Spirit. The three are one.

    (C) can be in two places at the same time. He is everywhere.

___ 10. Jesus Christ . . .

    (A) is the only way to heaven.

    (B) was a good man, a prophet, not divine.

    (C) is the Messiah.

___ 11. The Holy Spirit . . .

    (A) is the person of God who indwells all Christians.

(B) is a real person with whom one can talk and receive guidance.

(C) refers to the power of God, not an actual person.

___ 12. Hell . . .

(A) does not really exist.

(B) is an actual place.

(C) exists now, on earth.

___ 13. Satan . . .

(A) does not really exist.

(B) is a fallen angel who seeks to destroy man.

(C) and his demonic power over man were defeated by the blood of Jesus Christ.

CLOSING DEVOTION
STARS

Take turns reading as we learn about having a more intimate time with God in our daily quiet time.

READER ONE: To help us develop a more intimate, personal relationship with God, let's look at a devotion called STARS. The "S" stands for "singing." Remember how we are told to enter into His presence with singing and be thankful unto Him (Ps. 100:2). We should find a quiet place, where we can be alone with God, hold the Bible in our hands, close our eyes, and sing aloud or in our spirit. Inside ourselves, we can sing praises unto God. Sing whatever comes to mind. Sing and become lost in time, praising and worshiping our Heavenly Father. Draw near unto Him.

READER TWO: The "T" naturally stands for "thankful." When the singing within us has stopped, we should begin to thank Him. Thank Him for our life, for our health, for our loved ones. Thank Him for whatever comes to mind. Love Him and thank Him for His goodness.

READER THREE: Now we move to "A"—"ask Him." Here we must ask Him to forgive us for whatever sins we have committed. Ask Him for the things we need. Ask Him for the needs of others. We need to just open up and talk with Him, discuss our problems

	and our plans with Him. We should think through our plans with the Lord, asking Him any specific questions we may have, allowing our minds to meditate, to clarify, and to be receptive to His thoughts. Think about, "What would happen if . . ." We should think through our plans allowing God's Holy Spirit to guide us.
READER FOUR:	"R" stands for "read." Each day during our time in the STARS, we should read and study His Word. It may be only a chapter a day, but we need to be consistent and read His Word daily. It is good to have a set path of Bible study. It is also good to remain flexible and allow the Holy Spirit to guide our thoughts to specific Scripture verses that we have learned. Do not, however, play "Bible Roulette" and simply open the Bible and point to a Scripture. God does not want us to treat Him like a fortune cookie.
READER FIVE:	Lastly, as we come to the close of our quiet time in the STARS, we should close our eyes and sing His praises once again. If we will follow this path through the STARS, we will be drawn into a close personal relationship with Him. In this way, we will find the guidance, the direction, and the strength we need.
READER SIX:	(Closing Prayer)

Chapter 12

CARE to Confront

K en and his wife, Sheila, were active members of their church. Ken headed the fund-raising drive one year and was on the building committee. Sheila participated in the women's circle and delivered food to people for Meals on Wheels.

As prominent members of the community, Ken and Sheila also enjoyed an active social life. Ken was a successful businessman, and they frequently entertained friends and clients. They typically served alcohol at their parties. Ken would have a drink at lunch, either to relax or to try to loosen up his business prospects. Sheila and Ken would sometimes have a couple of drinks at night at home together or at the club when they went out for dinner. A glass of wine at dinner kept the romance alive.

No one ever said anything to Ken about his drinking. It seemed excessive at times, but normal.

Ken's company initiated a business deal one fall that kept him traveling to a nearby community. As the project was getting off the ground, Ken would take the sales crew out for drinks and partying. During these trips, Ken got to know, and ultimately became sexually involved with, a young woman on the sales staff.

Close Christian friends of Ken's and Sheila's became aware of Ken's double life. They also watched Ken change. Some of Ken's Christian male friends noticed Ken's language and interests and attitudes become more sensual, but they never confronted him. They chose not to get involved.

Ken finally divorced Sheila and moved to the nearby town. He never goes to church anymore and has lost contact with the Christian men he used to call his friends. Sheila no longer sees her Christian girlfriends either. They've dropped her since the divorce. They don't mean to ignore her—it's just that she is single and doesn't seem to fit in anymore.

AM I MY BROTHER'S KEEPER?

The world prefers that people mind their own business. Many times, Christians fall into this worldly thinking and isolate themselves from those who fall into sin, or, as with Ken's friends, they look the other way.

This "don't get involved" attitude is made worse by the "do your own thing" mentality of the many non-Christian secular counselors. These counselors lack the absolute guiding principles of the Bible and distort the principle of acceptance into condoning almost any behavior chosen by two consenting adults. These counselors often have no direction in which to lead people. They believe that each man should find his own truth from within.

As Christians, we have the truth. There are absolutes regarding behavior, attitudes, and relationships. The Word of God also tells us we have a responsibility to care enough for each other that when we see a brother or sister in error, we should confront his sinful behavior, language, and attitudes. In Matthew 18:15–20 we read that if a man sees his brother committing a sin, he should go to his brother and confront him. If the brother will not listen, the man should take another brother with him and confront the brother who is in sin. If the brother still will not listen, the matter should be brought to the church.

Unfortunately, Ken and Sheila's Christian friends failed to confront Ken. They didn't want to get involved. How often we see this in the church today!

Sometimes we confuse confrontation with judgment, and thus misapply Jesus' statement, "Judge not, that you be not judged" (Matt. 7:1). Certainly Scripture tells us not to judge or condemn our neighbors (James 4:11–12). However, there are also Scriptures that tell us to have judgment concerning the behavior of fellow believers and to confront sinful behavior. Note the guidance Paul gave the church in 1 Corinthians 5 for confronting the sexual immorality of certain members of the church. Consider also the example of Jesus.

Remember the story of the woman caught in the act of adultery? Jesus loved the sinner, but He always called the sinner to obey God's Word, to go and sin no more. Jesus was not soft on sin and neither should we. Following the example of Jesus, we need to love and accept all people, but not all behavior. Instead, we must appropriately confront sinful behavior, trusting the Holy Spirit to convict the person of his sin. We can then lovingly lead others to repent and receive forgiveness through Jesus Christ.

As Christian counselors and helping friends we have learned to introduce people to Jesus Christ and His Holy Spirit in a natural, nonthreatening way. Now, we will look at the fourth phase of the integrated counseling model, and using the word picture CARE, we will learn to confront a person's behavior and to help him change.

We certainly can all relate to the struggle with behavior. Even the apostle Paul struggled with his behavior as seen in his writings: "For what I will to do, that I do not practice; but what I hate, that I do" (Rom. 7:15).

The world and our flesh pull us in one direction. God's Word and His Holy Spirit lead us in another direction. How can we control our behavior? How can we successfully deal with sin and temptation? How can we confront another and lovingly help him to walk in obedience to Christ?

It all begins with a thought.

Chris, the College Student

Chris is a college student, lonely, insecure, away from home for the first time. Although he is a Christian, Chris has ignored personal Bible study and prayer since he has been at school. I need some time to settle in to school, he thought the day he arrived on campus. As soon as I get my schedule worked out and meet some friends, I can look for a church. I'm okay for now.

Chris has entered the second semester of college and is still not attending church or any Christian fellowship groups. He has not developed any Christian friendships. Instead, he has been drinking a little and running around with friends who are partying and sexually active. His friends have piles of *Playboy* and other similar magazines in their rooms. And in the last few months, he has begun to struggle with the sin of pornography and masturbation.

Time after time, Chris throws the magazines away and cries out to God for forgiveness. He promises God, "I will never do this again." Then, after a while, he falls back into his sinful pattern. Chris has become a carnal Christian, struggling and alone. But he doesn't have to stay as he is.

Self-effort or Surrender to God

Chris can have victory over temptation and sin. He does not have to be alone. God has promised that His Holy Spirit will live in us and be our Comforter and Counselor if we will turn to Him. He will be our constant companion and friend to help us in times of need, if we will talk to Him and relate to Him as a real person. God has also promised in Scripture: "No temptation has overtaken you except such as is common to man; but God is faithful, who will not allow you to be tempted beyond what you are able, but with the temptation will also make a way of escape, that you may be able to bear it" (1 Cor. 10:13).

As a Christian, Chris can believe and trust these promises. If he will memorize the verse from 1 Corinthians, bury it in his heart, and when tempted, turn to it for strength, he will feel God's presence. God, after all, promises in the verse to help us when tempted. He has given us His Holy Spirit to help us to live a new and transformed life. But Chris has become double-minded—he has moved away from God and has begun to rely on his own strength to change. And it all started with his thought life: I can make it on my own.

Chris promises God, "I will never do this again," which is an important commitment. But the spirit is willing and the flesh is weak. Self-effort is not strong enough to turn away temptation and sin.

There are physical things Chris needs to do. He needs to destroy the pornography in his possession. He needs to stay away from sources of pornography. He needs to get involved with Christian groups and a church. He needs to cultivate Christian friends. He needs to pray and turn to God when temptation comes.

Only through a surrendered relationship to the Holy Spirit can a person have true victory over temptation and sin. It works the same way for adults. Notice what happens when the pastor's wife does not control her thought life.

Pat and Ted

Ted was a pastor at First Church in Small Town, Colorado. Pat, his wife, was not very happy living in Small Town. But she supported Ted's desire to have his own church and understood that, like all young pastors, he had to go through the ranks. When Ted reached forty-five years old and the Bishop passed him over for promotion, Pat began to get restless.

Pat longed for the glamorous active life of a big city, like Denver, where she grew up. So she was excited when Ted promised to take her to Denver for her twentieth high school reunion.

The reunion began with a cocktail party at six in the evening at the Country Club. There were heavy hors d'oeuvres, but no dinner. The party continued on into the night, with a band and dancing. Pat was excited about seeing all of her old high school friends, many of whom still lived in Denver. It seemed like everyone was trying to relive their teenage years, especially Pat, who spent most of the night dancing with Mike, her high school sweetheart.

Ted tried to get Pat to leave around eleven. After all, it was a long drive back to Small Town and Ted had to preach the next morning. But Pat insisted on staying. She told Ted that one of her friends, Helen, had invited her to stay over. So finally, Ted went home alone.

By late Sunday evening Ted still hadn't heard from Pat. He called his mother-in-law to get Helen's last name and telephone number. He called Helen and learned that Pat had not gone home with her after the party. Ted then got Mike's number and called his apartment. Pat answered the telephone.

Pat never came home. She divorced Ted and married Mike.

Pat had been a faithful pastor's wife. She had taught a fourth-grade Sunday school class, helped out at the church coffees, and taught couples' Bible studies with her husband. Who would have thought that all of a sudden, in a weekend, she could leave her husband, leave the church, and move in with her old boyfriend? It happened, but not all of a sudden.

In her thoughts, Pat had longed for another life. For more than five years, she found some of the glamor she was looking for in the soap operas she was addicted to. And for a year, since she first received the letter about the high school reunion, Pat had been thinking about Mike. Helen had written to her and told her about Mike's divorce and about how good looking he still was. Mentally, emotionally, and spiritually, Pat had been leaving her husband for a long time.

With Chris, the college student, and Pat, the pastor's wife, the problem was in their thought life. Their thoughts led them away from God and into temptation and sin.

Our thought lives create the fantasies and imaginations and desires in our heart. If we dwell on sinful thoughts, they will lead us ultimately to commit the sinful act or behavior. We begin by foolishly believing we can fantasize or sin just a little and get away with it. We stand in the strength that the Holy Spirit gives us and tease and play around with sin. In doing so we destroy the powerful intimate relationship we have with God. We become weak and vulnerable to further temptation. And if we continue to play with the temptation, we will "get hooked" on its pleasure, as did Chris and Pat, and Satan will "reel" us into deeper sin.

THE MASTER SALESMAN

Satan is a master salesman for the product of sin. The author of deception, he peddles his product with false advertising and a keen eye for opportunity. He makes sin sound acceptable, even appealing. He holds it out to us, promising pleasure and excitement. He changes its name, disguising the evil and promoting the glamor, power, and pleasure. The sin of adultery is called "having an affair," as if someone were hosting a grand party. The sin of fornication is said to be "making love" or "living together." The sin of homosexuality is called an "alternative life-style," and the homosexual is referred to as being "gay." An unborn baby is killed, and it is said the "pregnancy has been terminated."

Satan twists our thinking. He is out to convince us that neither he, nor hell, nor sin really exist. "There is nothing to fear. If it feels good, do it," he says. And sin does feel good—for a while.

But in fact, sin is the source of pain—the disease itself. The love Satan sells is lust—an emotional lie. Satan's joy is chemically induced; it comes in a bottle and leaves you hung over. The fun-filled pain relievers of this fallen angel offer nothing more than emptiness, heartache, and hell. Sin is tempting, but it really does not meet our needs or deliver what it promises.

Satan is also a great opportunist. He always knows when we are tired, hurting, discouraged, lonely, and vulnerable for his sales pitch.

The Price of a Drink

Imagine for a moment walking across the desert. You are hot, tired, and thirsty. All you can think about is how good it would be to have a tall, cool drink.

Lucifer, the snake-oil salesman, suddenly appears with a bottle of his delicious new refreshment drink called S*I*N. He pours it over ice with a big lemon on the side and offers it to you.

You see the label marked Deadly Poison, but you are so thirsty! The drink fizzes and pops and sparkles. There are others there, drinking in S*I*N. They are laughing and having fun. The S*I*N doesn't seem to bother them. Could the label be wrong?

Are you going to drink from that cool refreshing beverage, enjoy that mouth-watering taste—and die from its poison? Or are you going to ignore the lies of that snake-oil salesman, refuse to look upon his icy beverage, tell him to flee from you, and walk into the burning sands?

Stop! S*I*N is poison. It refreshes for a moment, but it brings death. Many knowingly gulp it down. They don't want to believe the label. They are in a hurry to take away the pain. They want relief now! They don't want to deny themselves that moment of pleasure. Yet, they drink to their death.

Satan comes to us when we are vulnerable and hurting and in our own desert. He offers a quick fix to take away the pain, to replace the ache with pleasure. He knows how to appeal to us. He knows how to confuse our thoughts and feed us lies so we will succumb to the fantasies or imaginations we have been nurturing. Consider Eve.

Temptation of Eve

Satan started tempting mankind with Eve. And he began by misdirecting her thoughts.

In the garden (Genesis 3), Satan, the serpent, went to Eve and said,

> *"Has God indeed said, 'You shall not eat of every tree in the garden'?" And the woman said to the serpent, "We may eat the fruit of the trees of the garden; but of the fruit of the tree which is in the midst of the garden, God has said, 'You shall not eat it, nor shall you touch it, lest you die.'"*
>
> *Then the serpent said to the woman, "You will not surely die. For God knows that in the day you eat of it your eyes will be opened, and you will be like God, knowing good and evil."*

Satan lied to Eve and tempted her spiritually. "You will be like God," he said.

> *So when the woman saw that the tree was good for food [physical temptation], that it was pleasant to the eyes [emotional temptation], and a tree desirable to make one wise [mental temptation], she took of its fruit and ate.*

Satan did not stop with Eve, of course. He has kept up his work through the ages. He even tried to take on Jesus, as seen in Matthew 4:1–10.

Then Jesus was led up by the Spirit into the wilderness to be tempted by the devil. And when He had fasted forty days and forty nights, afterward He was hungry. Now when the tempter came to Him, he said, "If You are the Son of God, command that these stones become bread" [physical temptation].

But He answered and said, "It is written: 'Man shall not live by bread alone, but by every word that proceeds from the mouth of God.'"

Then the devil took Him up into the holy city, set Him on the pinnacle of the temple, and said to Him, "If You are the Son of God, throw Yourself down [an attempt to pull Jesus off balance emotionally, basically telling Jesus to prove that He is the Son of God]. *For it is written:*

'He shall give His angels charge over you,'
and,
'In their hands they shall bear you up,
Lest you dash your foot against a stone.'" [This was an intellectual test of scriptural understanding.]

Jesus said to him, "It is written again, 'You shall not tempt the LORD your God.'"

Again, the devil took Him up on an exceedingly high mountain, and showed Him all the kingdoms of the world and their glory. And he said to Him, "All these things I will give You if You will bow down and worship me" [spiritual temptation].

Then Jesus said to him, "Away with you, Satan! For it is written: 'You shall worship the LORD your God, and Him only you shall serve.'"

Satan tempted Jesus in body, soul (mind and emotions), and spirit, just as he had tempted Eve.

Many people in the time of Jesus and today think of sin as

only a physical act. They do not consider the above passages that show that sin can also be committed in the soul (mind and emotions). In fact, throughout the Bible sin is associated with the soul (mind and emotions), as well as the flesh. God destroyed the world with the flood because,

> The LORD saw that the wickedness of man was great in the earth [physical, body], and that every intent of the thoughts of his heart [soul] was only evil continually (Gen. 6:5 emphasis added).

> For the word of God is living and powerful, and sharper than any two-edged sword, piercing even to the division of soul and spirit, and of joints and marrow [body], and is a discerner of the thoughts [mind] and intents of the heart [emotions] (Heb. 4:12).

We must control our thoughts to live the Christian life. Typically when we try to change some sinful addictive behavior in our lives, we first attempt to change that behavior physically. We quit the act. We throw away the cigarettes, pour out the booze, or break off the affair. Yet, how often do we, like Chris, take the first step and, after a while, slip back into our old habits?

We must take this first step of removing ourselves physically from the temptation and from where others are engaged in the behavior. But then, we must remove the temptation from our thought lives. We must control our thoughts.

REMOVE THE DESIRE

The mind is a marvelous thing. It stores in its memory not only the facts, but the feelings. If we dwell on an event in our thoughts, we will soon begin to experience the same feelings and desires we had when the event occurred. If we dwell in our minds on old habits or sinful behavior, Satan will repeat his old lies and the temptation will return. The desire to sin will grow.

We must refuse, refuse, refuse to fantasize or think about that former behavior. Instead, we need to pray and ask God to cleanse our hearts and to remove the sinful desire. Then we need to be continually submitted to God. Refuse to think sinful thoughts. Refuse to think about the sinful behavior.

James 4:7–8 says, "*Submit* yourselves therefore to God. *Resist* the devil, and he will flee from you. *Draw nigh* to God, and he will draw nigh to you" (KJV emphasis added). As Christians we do not have to be controlled by our flesh, by lustful desires and sinful thoughts. We have been set free from the control sin once had over our lives. Now, when we submit to God, we will be successful in resisting the devil because we are acting in the power of God. After the temptation has passed, we draw near to God, and there we will be comforted, loved, strengthened, and reassured as God draws nigh unto us.

Once we have submitted and committed to God, we need to replace sinful behavior with constructive behavior.

The eyes are the window of the soul. We must be careful about what we watch on television and about what we read. Temptation is everywhere. Satan will try to stir up old desires through television, magazines, movies, books, newspapers, the attitudes of other people. We need to ask, "How much time do I spend with the things of the world, and how much time do I spend studying God's Word? How much time do I spend in prayer?"

Then we need to fill up that empty time! As we stop reading sinful books, we should start reading the Bible and other constructive material. We need to fill our lives with good, wholesome, healthy, holy thoughts like those found in these Scripture passages.

And do not be not conformed to this world, but be transformed by the renewing of your mind, *that you may prove what is that good and acceptable and perfect will of God (Rom. 12:2 emphasis added).*

Casting down imaginations, *and every high thing that exalteth itself against the knowledge of God, and bringing into captivity* every thought *to the obedience of Christ (2 Cor. 10:5 KJV emphasis added).*

Finally, brethren, whatever things are true, whatever things are noble, whatever things are just, whatever things are pure, whatever things are lovely, whatever things are of good report, if there is any virtue and if there is anything praiseworthy—meditate on these things *(Phil. 4:8 emphasis added).*

Commit your works to the LORD, / And your thoughts will be established (Prov. 16:3 emphasis added).

As we leave the company of friends involved in sinful behavior, we need to replace those old friends with new Christian friends.

God does not snap His fingers and change us. He allows us to have control over our behavior and thought lives. He allows us to have a free will, to make choices.

Our hearts, our innermost desires, will only change as we surrender our body and soul (mind and emotions) completely and continually to the Holy Spirit. As this occurs, the desire to pursue destructive, addictive, or sinful behavior will go away. Then we will have abiding victory deep in our soul, victory over the desire to sin and dominion over the flesh. We will experience joy and inner peace because we finally have control over our thought lives and no longer repeat the former sins.

Understanding our own struggle with behavior and need to control our thought lives makes us more compassionate as we reach out to others who are struggling. Confrontation is never easy, but realizing our own weaknesses enables us to identify and accept people.

SO HOW CAN I HELP SOMEONE WITH HIS BEHAVIOR?

Using the personal counseling model, you have met your hurting friend where he is, helped him with his problem, introduced him to Jesus through his general admission of sin, and introduced him to the Holy Spirit. Now you are ready to address any specific behavior you may be concerned about. You will be far more successful in bringing about a change in life-style or behavior now that the person has come to Christ, because apart from Christ and the Holy Spirit, the person does not have the power to change successfully or for the long-term. He may successfully overcome one addictive behavior only to pick up another. He may change one sin for another. It's like changing rooms on the *Titanic*. To become a new creation, we must come to Jesus Christ and obey His Holy Spirit.

The Holy Spirit convicts us of our sin and reveals the truth to us. And the Holy Spirit gives us the power to live a new and transformed life. After the person comes to Christ, he will be able to make behavioral changes because he will have the Holy Spirit within himself. God does not require that a person overcome his sins before coming to Him. Once the person commits his life to Christ and seeks to live for God, the Holy Spirit will give him the knowledge and the power to live according to God's Holy Word.

In counseling with Christians regarding their personal behavior, you must:

C—*Confront* his sinful behavior.

A—Help him become *aware* of what God's Word says about that specific behavior. Allow him to read a Scripture about that behavior out loud and ask him to explain its meaning. In this way, you do not come across as being "preachy" and the Holy Spirit has the opportunity to reveal the truth to him.

R—Lead him to *repent*. Encourage the person to take the step (to turn to Christ, to discontinue certain behavior), but do not manipulate or push him or he will say things only to please you. If this happens, he has not made a commitment to change, even though he may have said the "right" words.

E —*Encourage* the person to seek a living relationship with the Holy Spirit and to actively read and study the Word of God. This is the best way for a person to be assured that his thought life, desires, and behavior will change.

Confront the Behavior

As Christian counselors and friends, Jesus is our model counselor. We want to observe how Jesus counseled and helped people and go and do likewise. Jesus loved the sinner and confronted sinful behavior; so must we!

The following guidelines will prove helpful for confronting sinful behavior:

1. **Acceptance:** Does the person sense that he is cared about and accepted as a person? Without the establishment of a feeling of personal acceptance and concern, a confrontation about behavior may be perceived as personal rejection and condemnation.

2. **Empathy:** Does the person sense that you understand his attitude, behavior, and life-style? If he doesn't feel understood, he may not be willing to seriously consider the confrontation.

3. **Timing:** Does the person have a high anxiety level? There may be several immediate problems that must be dealt with before deeper issues can be confronted. He also may need to talk for a while, to release tension, and to solve some other problems before he is willing to confront the destructive behavior.

4. **Attitude:** What is the person's attitude toward change? Does he acknowledge that the behavior is causing some problems? Recognition of the problem is the first step toward change.

5. **Concise:** Any confrontation should be concisely stated. A wordy confrontation becomes a lecture.

6. **Leading:** The confrontation may be phrased as a leading question, encouraging the person to express his beliefs and attitudes.

   For Example: "Sandra, what do you think about living with Tom and not being married?"

Be sure to confront with the word *think* and not *feel*. The sin may feel good, though the person knows that it is wrong.

Changing Behavior

The following steps outline the path to changing behavior, to changing lives:

1. Acknowledge that a problem exists and that changes need to occur.

2. Assume responsibility for the problem—"I need to change"—and commit to change.

3. Confess general sin to God, acknowledging that the penalty for sin is death.

4. Acknowledge that Jesus died in payment for your sin, and ask God to forgive you of your sin in the name of Jesus Christ.

5. Accept Jesus Christ as your personal Savior.

6. Ask God's Holy Spirit to take control of your life, and establish a close relationship with Him.

7. Repent and turn away from the sinful/destructive behavior, making a firm decision never to repeat the sinful/destructive behavior.

8. Ask God to bind Satan and the forces of evil from attacking you in that area of your life.

9. Avoid temptation. Realize that you must exercise your free will and choose to turn away from sin.

10. Let the mind that is in Christ Jesus dwell in you. Refuse to think sinful thoughts or to think about past sinful behavior. And instead, change your thoughts. Think about what is good and right and pure and holy. You can control your thoughts!

11. Study the Bible. Set aside a specific time each day to study God's Word.

12. Memorize Scripture and call forth that Scripture when temptation comes.

13. Obey God's Word.

14. Substitute holy, healthy activity for sinful, destructive activity. Stay busy.

15. Join a Bible teaching Christian church that is alive—where God is praised, where Jesus is lifted up, and where the Holy Spirit is openly and actively working in the lives of the people.

16. Live for Jesus. Put God first in your life. Trust Him to take care of you.

17. Serve others in personal ministry. Give your time, your talent, and your tithe to the church and to other Christian ministries. Get involved, volunteer.

18. Study and prepare yourself to serve others, learning how to share the love of God and His plan of forgiveness and salvation through Jesus Christ.

19. Share your new life with family and friends and make new Christian friends.

20. Go and make disciples, teaching others all God has revealed to you.

If someone you know is struggling to change his life or change some specific behavior, he may review these twenty steps and see where he is along the path toward change. Deep within, we can have great hope and assurance of achieving change as we claim God's promise: "I can do all things through Christ who strengthens me" (Phil. 4:13).

There is no limit to what God can do in our lives when we are submitted to Him. There is no sin, no habit, no destructive behavior too powerful for the power of God to overcome, if we seek to make these changes in our lives. The power of God is greater than the power of alcohol or drugs or sexual immorality or any other sin or destructive behavior. At the same time, God will not break our free will or force us to change. We must want to come to Him and want to change. If we will repent and express the desire to change, and confess our sin to God in the name of Jesus Christ, God promises to forgive, to cleanse, and to protect us from sin:

If we confess our sins, He is faithful and just to forgive us our sins and to cleanse us from all unrighteousness (1 John 1:9).

No temptation has overtaken you except such as is common to man; but God is faithful, who will not allow you to be tempted beyond what you are able, but with the

*temptation will also make the way of escape that you
may be able to bear it (1 Cor. 10:13).*

We will see in the next chapter how you can lead someone
who has slipped in his walk of faith to repentance—the R of
CARE.

CLOSING DEVOTION
If You Love Me

God does not play Walt Disney, touch us with a magic wand, and turn us into Snow White or Prince Charming. The wonderful thing about our relationship with God is that it is real. He loves us and wants to forgive us if we will come to Him. He died and paid for our sins, and He will come and live in us and give us the power to live a new and transformed life.

We receive power when His Holy Spirit comes upon us (see Acts 1:8), but He does not take over. God does not take away our free will. We are still free to make choices. In allowing us to be free, God gives us the opportunity to give Him the greatest gift of all.

Think for a moment about giving something to God. What can we possibly give to God? Can we give a chest full of gold to to the One who makes sunsets? Can we give diamonds to the One who made stars? What can we possibly give to God that would have any value?

God has so structured life and our relationship with Him that we have the opportunity to give God the most valuable gift of all—love.

Jesus said, "If you love Me, keep My commandments" (John 14:15).

"And you shall love the LORD your God with all your heart, with all your soul, with all your mind, and with all your strength. . . . You shall love your neighbor as yourself" (Mark 12:30–31).

"A new commandment I give to you, that you love one another; as I have loved you, that you also love one an-

*other. By this all will know that you are My disciples,
if you have love for one another" (John 13:34–35).*

Closing Prayer

Chapter 13

Follow CHRIST: Volunteer and Serve Him

It's not enough to go to church, put your money in the plate, and go home.

God wants our time and our talents in Christian service, as well as our personal worship and stewardship. We are called to be "doers of the word, and not hearers only" (James 1:22). We are a nation of priests, where every Christian is called into the ministry.

As a Christian counselor or helping friend, your ultimate goal is to encourage the person you have helped to become a doer of the Word. And he can do this by developing a personal ministry in which he can reach out to others, just as you have reached out to him.

It is in CHRIST that we have our ministry. As we saw in chapter 2 of the book, CHRIST stands for

C—*Commitment!* God calls us to make a deep commitment. "Take up your cross," Jesus said. There is a cost in being a disciple.

H—His *Holy Spirit* will go with us, however. He must truly be in control of our lives. We must

R—*Read* and study God's Word,

I—*Involve* Jesus in all of our decisions; intercede for others, and go forth

S—*Serving* others,

T—*Teaching* and sharing with them all that God has revealed to us.

We do not have to have degrees in psychology or theology to have a personal ministry. Personal ministry means getting involved personally. Every day opportunities present themselves for us to become involved. We simply need to have our eyes open to what they are.

At the end of this chapter, you will find an interest assessment, which you can take yourself, or give to someone you are helping. This will help you become aware of ways you can begin to minister in your church.

If we take up our cross and follow CHRIST, committing our time and our talents, there is no limit to what God can do through us. His Holy Spirit will direct us; we will gain the insight and wisdom we need from His Word. And as we pray for others we will see how we can serve and teach others what God has taught us.

Let's consider the characteristics of someone who was willing to go out of the way to get involved.

THE GOOD SAMARITAN

"An expert in the law stood up to test Jesus one day. 'Teacher,' he asked, 'what must I do to inherit eternal life?'

'What is written in the law?' Jesus responded. 'How do you read it?' [Notice the counseling technique Jesus used. Jesus redirected the question back to him.]

He answered, 'Love the Lord your God with all your

*heart and all your soul and with all your strength and with
all your mind and love your neighbor as yourself.'*

*'You have answered correctly,' Jesus replied. 'Do this and
you will live.'*

*But he wanted to justify himself, so he asked Jesus, 'And
who is my neighbor?'*

*In reply Jesus said, 'A man was going down from
Jerusalem to Jericho, when he fell into the hands of robbers.
They stripped him of his clothes, beat him, and went away,
leaving him half dead.*

*'A priest happened to be going down the road, and when
he saw the man, he passed by on the other side. So too, a
Levite, when he came to the place and saw him, passed by
on the other side. But a Samaritan, as he traveled, came
where the man was, and when he saw him, he took pity on
him. He went to him and bandaged his wounds, pouring on
oil and wine. Then he put the man on his own donkey, took
him to an inn and took care of him.*

*'The next day he took out two silver coins and gave them
to the innkeeper. "Look after him," he said. "And when I
return, I will reimburse you for any extra expenses you may
have."*

*'Which of these three do you think was a neighbor to the
man who fell into the hands of the robbers?'*

*The expert in the law replied, 'The one who had mercy
on him.'*

Jesus told him, 'Go and do likewise.' "

Luke 10:25–37 (paraphrased)

In the story of the Good Samaritan, the church is represented by the priest, and religious people are represented by the
Levite. Both saw the injured man, yet neither got involved. Instead, they walked by on the other side of the road.

Unfortunately, today, just as two thousand years ago, many

Christians are walking by on the other side of the road. We are aware of the problems in our society, but we choose not to get involved.

Jesus held the Samaritan up as an example for us when He said, "Go and do likewise." What did the Good Samaritan do that we should emulate?

1. He saw the person in need and set aside his work to stop and help. We must be aware of those around us and willing to place the needs of others before our own.

2. He was moved with compassion. We must truly care about other people and their needs and take action.

3. He became physically and personally involved. Christians must be willing to become physically and personally involved in helping other people.

4. He was willing to be personally inconvenienced. He put the man on his animal, which means that the Good Samaritan had to walk into town. Sometimes we must endure inconvenience when we stop to help someone.

5. He did not stop with just the immediate need. He continued to meet needs in providing shelter, food, and personal care. We are called to go beyond a small handout and provide in-depth help.

6. He reached into his pocket and gave financially. He even pledged future support. Christians should give unselfishly. It is Scriptural to make financial commitments regarding future ministry needs.

7. He got other people involved. Christians need to work together in ministry.

8. He promised to return and follow up. Christians should follow through and seek to establish a continuing relationship with those they are helping.

All we have to do is look around us and we will see people in need, longing for someone to reach out and help. We can follow the example of the Good Samaritan in simple ways, every day, on our own. Or we can choose to become involved in something as time consuming as starting a telephone helpline ministry. (See Appendix Three for more information on the benefits of a helpline and how to start one.)

The following are ways you can imitate the example of the Good Samaritan on your own:

- Bake a cake and take it to the family that has just moved into the neighborhood. Invite them to go to church with you.
- Be sensitive to the people at work. When you notice stress and anxiety, invite the person to lunch and listen.
- Take the initiative and reach out to friends going through a crisis. Call them on the phone. Tell them you love them. Ask them how they are and what they have been doing. Listen to them.
- Invite your pastor and his family to dinner.
- Volunteer to help out in the church office.
- Serve as a volunteer on the telephone helpline.
- Teach a Sunday school class.
- Work with the Boy Scouts.
- Visit those in prison or those in the nursing home.

You can develop a personal ministry through acts as simple as these, or you can become a volunteer in a parachurch ministry such as Meals on Wheels or serve on your church visitation team.

God has given us different gifts, abilities, skills, and personalities. So that you may find the ministry area of greatest interest to you, please complete the personal assessment on page 251.

If you are part of a group, turn this in to your group leader. If you are working through this book on your own, take your assessment to someone on the staff of your church. Let them know you want to become involved, serving the people in your church, and ask them what ministries are available for you to do this.

Explore the parachurch ministries in your community, find out if your church helps finance any of these ministries, or if any members are actively involved as volunteers and as board members. You may be able to help the members of your church become involved in a local ministry. Perhaps you will even help your church start a ministry.

The opportunities are endless. When you step out to serve God, His Holy Spirit will fill you and minister through you. Experience the power and presence of God in your life as you volunteer and serve Him.

CLOSING DEVOTION
Reach Out and Help

As you have read through this text, it is my prayer that you have heard the call to ministry and found the insight you need to reach out and help those in need. With the principles of the personal counseling model you can follow Jesus' example, accepting and focusing on the people you counsel, helping with their problem, leading them into a relationship with Jesus Christ and the Holy Spirit, confronting their behavior and encouraging them to be faithful disciples of Christ, and helping them to develop a ministry. As you put these principles into practice, you will be fulfilling your call to be a fisher of men.

We are the disciples of today. It is our responsibility to carry the Gospel to this generation, but we are not alone. The Holy Spirit of God goes with us. He has a plan and a purpose for our lives. We must be sensitive to His guidance each day as He seeks to minister to people through us. We have the awesome privilege of loving the unlovable, helping the helpless, and ministering to those around us under the power and anointing of the Holy Spirit in the name of Jesus Christ.

There is no limit to what God can do through us. We have been called and we have been chosen as the modern-day disciples of Jesus Christ. May all that we do be pleasing in His sight.

COURSE REVIEW

Name _____

Date _____

Group Leader _____

Complete this review and see how much you have learned.

1. Outline the counseling model (5 P's).

    (1) _____

    (2) _____

    (3) _____   _____

    (4) _____   _____

    (5) _____   _____

2. Outline the picture word and meaning (Phase One):

    (1) _____

    (2) _____

    (3) _____

    (4) _____

3. Outline the picture word and meaning (Phase Two):

    (1) _____

    (2) _____

    (3) _____

    (4) _____

4. Outline the picture word and meaning (Phase Three):

    (1) _____

    (2) _____

(3) _____

(4) _____

5. Outline the picture word and meaning (Phase Four):

(1) _____

(2) _____

(3) _____

(4) _____

6. Outline the picture word and meaning (Phase Five):

(1) _____

(2) _____

(3) _____

(4) _____

(5) _____

(6) _____

Write the requested response to each of the following:

7. **Man:** I've tried to find a job. I just can't find anything.

   Open-ended Question _____

   _____

   _____

   _____

8. **Young Girl:** Bob has asked me to marry him.

   Open-ended Question _____

   _____

   _____

   _____

9. **Girl:** I'm at my wit's end.

   Open-ended Question _____

_____

_____

_____

10. **Woman:** My boss said I will have to move to Jacksonville if I want to get into the training program.

   Open-ended Question _____

   _____

   _____

   _____

11. **Elderly Lady:** I've been so lonesome since my husband died.

   Feeling _____

   _____

   _____

   _____

12. **College Student:** I can't seem to cope anymore.

   Mirror _____

   _____

   _____

   _____

13. **Woman:** My husband hit me again. He's been drinking.

   Crisis Intervention _____

   _____

   _____

   _____

14. **Young Girl:** What do you do when nobody cares?

   Feeling _____

   _____

   _____

   _____

15. **Woman:** My husband moved out. He said he doesn't love me anymore.

    Content _____

    _____

    _____

    _____

16. **Close Friend:** I saw the doctor today. I have cancer. They are going to operate Wednesday, and I want you to have my stamp collection.

    Content _____

    _____

    _____

    _____

17. **Sister:** I found drugs in Billy's room. I don't know what to do. I'm afraid if I say anything, he'll run away.

    Content _____

    _____

    _____

    _____

18. **Spouse:** Honey, sit down. Our daughter is pregnant and she is going to have an abortion.

    _____

    _____

    _____

19. **Spouse:** Honey, Mama just died . . . (crying)

    _____

    _____

    _____

20. **Son:** Mom, Dad, we are going to get married.

    _____

    _____

    _____

21. Write out Diagnostic Question Number One.

_____

_____

_____

_____

_____

22. Write out Diagnostic Question Number Two.

_____

_____

_____

_____

_____

23. Outline the Home Run Presentation of the Gospel.

First Base _____

Second Base _____

Shortstop _____

Third Base _____

Home _____

24. Write out the Restaurant Story.

_____

_____

_____

_____

_____

_____

_____

_____

_____

_____

_____

_____

_____
_____
_____
_____
_____
_____
_____
_____
_____

25. Write out the Sinner's Prayer.

(1) _____
(2) _____
(3) _____
(4) _____
(5) _____
(6) _____
(7) _____
(8) _____

26. Write out the following Scripture verses.

1. John 14:16

_____
_____
_____
_____
_____
_____

2. John 14:26

_____
_____
_____
_____

_____

_____

3. Galatians 5:22

_____

_____

_____

_____

_____

4. 1 Corinthians 10:13

_____

_____

_____

_____

_____

27. Outline the Two Triangle Presentation and the column that accompanies the Two Triangle Presentation.

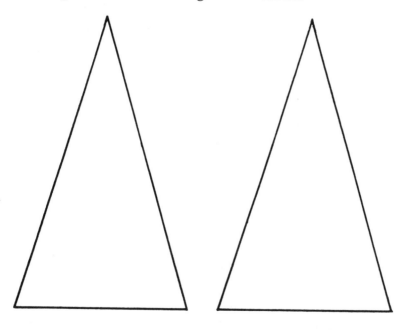

And this column that accompanies the Two Triangle
Presentation:

_____

_____

_____

_____

_____

_____

_____

Personal Assessment

1. List the types of activities you enjoy (work, hobbies, ministry).

   _____

   _____

   _____

   _____

   _____

2. Check the ministry areas in which you would like to serve:

___ Nursery	___ Office Volunteer	___ Telephone Counselor
___ Children	___ Accounting	___ Prayer Chain
___ Youth	___ Computer	___ Support Group
___ Singles	___ Bulletin	___ Peer Counselor
___ Usher	___ Newsletter	___ Home Visitation
___ Greeter	___ Bulk Mail	___ Hospital
___ Altar/Flowers	___ Notes/Cards	___ Nursing Home
___ Hospitality	___ Choir	___ Crisis Pregnancy
___ Food	___ Bell Choir	___ Food Ministry
___ Driver	___ Sound Dept.	___ Street Ministry
___ Repair/Clean	___ Band	___ Prison Ministry
___ Landscaping	___ Puppets	___ Divorce Recovery
___ Grief Support	___ Bible Study	___ Home Group
___ Sunday School	___ Prayer Group	___ Preaching
___ Teaching	___ Speaking	___ Evangelizing
___ Planning	___ Budgeting	___ Fund-raising

Other _____

_____

_____

_____

_____

How often would you be available to serve in one of these ministry areas? Check the spaces in the grid below.

	Sun	Mon	Tue	Wed	Thurs	Fri	Sat
Morning							
Afternoon							
Evening							

Appendices

PART THREE

Appendix 1

Course Syllabus

How Can I Help? is a course in personal Christian counseling that teaches a person how to reach out or respond when someone is in crisis. It presents a practical five-step counseling model that utilizes biblically based counseling principles and techniques, taking examples from the ministry of Jesus. It presents an overview of the basic tenets of the Christian faith and teaches a person how to introduce someone to Jesus Christ as his Savior in a natural, nonthreatening way and how to lead someone into a close relationship with the Holy Spirit. *How Can I Help?* is a course about life and how to handle the personal crisis situations that come into all of our lives.

COURSE OBJECTIVES

The objectives of this course are:

1. To give the student an understanding of personal crisis situations.

2. To help the student to understand the role of the personal counselor/helping friend.

3. To impart practical counseling skills to the student and build confidence through role play experience.

4. To communicate the personal command from Jesus that His followers should respond to people in personal crisis.

5. To teach the student how to go about solving problems.

6. To teach the student how to integrate his Christian faith into the personal counseling process, how to confront sinful behavior, and how to introduce a person to Jesus in a natural, nonthreatening way.

7. To confirm the student's understanding of the basic tenets of the Christian faith.

8. To teach the student how to resist temptation and sin and how to counsel with friends, helping them to change thoughts and behavior.

9. To inspire and challenge the student to answer the call of Christ to minister to others.

10. To "Go and make disciples."

INSTRUCTION METHODS

How Can I Help? is presented in lecture, along with counseling demonstrations. The class is organized into small groups under the guidance of Group Leaders who facilitate exercises and role play. Role play dramatizations present situations demonstrating the counseling skills and evangelism presentations.

Term Paper

Christian colleges teaching this course for academic credit require students to conduct research and write a term paper on one of the following topics:

Abortion	Homosexuality
Alcoholism	Loneliness
Battered Women	Marital Problems
Child Abuse	Mental & Emotional Problems
Dating, Love & Marriage	Rape
Divorce	Sexual Immorality
Drug Abuse	Street People
Grief	Suicide

Term Paper Guidelines

- Discuss the subject in general.
- Determine how critical the problem is locally.
- Compare the national trend over the past several years.
- Visit a local agency or support group that works in this area and discuss their services, hours, and fees.
- List five agencies of help to which a person with this problem could turn for help.
- In what way is the Christian community responding to this problem?
- What recommendations can be offered for an improved Christian response?

Student Ministry

Most Christian colleges, churches, helplines, and other ministries offering this course also provide the student with an opportunity for volunteer service where the student can practice his counseling and helping skills.

Texts

1. Holy Bible
2. *How Can I Help?* by W. H. "Skip" Hunt, Ph.D.

Appendix 2

Christian Helplines, Inc.

Christian Helplines, Inc. (CHI) is a national association of local Christian telephone counseling/crisis intervention ministries. The Member Centers of CHI are independent ministries that provide 24 hour Christian telephone counseling, prayer, crisis intervention, and referral information on churches and agencies of help in their local communities.

Some CHI Member Centers also operate crisis pregnancy centers, maternity homes, marriage and family counseling centers, food distribution centers, and other crisis programs. Some CHI centers operate specialized lines of help to teens, to pregnant women, and some operate prayer lines in conjunction with Christian television ministries or local churches. Some operate closely within a given church denomination. Most involve a number of local Christian churches working together.

All CHI Member Centers join together in a common mission, with common beliefs and standards, and a common commitment as expressed in the documents that follow. CHI has developed resources, i.e., manuals, videos, etc. to assist Christian groups in organizing and operating crisis ministries.

MISSION STATEMENT

Christian Helplines, Inc., and its member centers have a threefold mission of

- Training Christian laypeople to counsel and minister, following the example of Jesus Christ and the teaching of His Holy Bible;

- Providing Christian counseling services to the people of our communities; and

- Sharing the love of God, His plan of forgiveness and salvation through Jesus Christ, and the transforming power of His Holy Spirit with all who would receive Him, without imposing religious beliefs on anyone.

STATEMENT OF FAITH

WE BELIEVE the Bible to be the inspired, the only infallible, authoritative Word of God (2 Tim. 3:16; 2 Peter 1:20–21).

WE BELIEVE that there is one God, eternally existent in three persons: Father, Son, and Holy Spirit (Matt. 3:16–17).

WE BELIEVE in the deity of our Lord Jesus Christ, His virgin birth, His sinless life, His miracles, His substitutionary atoning death through His shed blood, His bodily resurrection, His ascension to the right hand of the Father, and His personal return in power and glory (Matt. 1:21–23; 3:17; 28:7; John 12:37; Acts 1:9–11; Heb. 4:15).

WE BELIEVE that for the salvation of lost and sinful man, regeneration by the Holy Spirit is absolutely essential (Titus 3:5).

WE BELIEVE that salvation is by grace through faith alone and not a result of any work (Eph. 2:8–9).

WE BELIEVE in the present ministry of the Holy Spirit by whose indwelling the Christian is enabled to live a godly life, is empowered to witness, and is given spiritual gifts for the common good of the Body of Christ, the Church (John 7:37–39; Acts 1:8; Gal. 5:22–23; 1 Cor. 12:4–7, 11; 1 Peter 4:10).

WE BELIEVE in the bodily resurrection of both the saved and the lost, those who are saved to the resurrection of eternal life, and those who are lost to the resurrection of eternal separation from God (1 Thess. 5:16–18; Rev. 20:11–15).

STANDARDS OF CHRISTIAN MINISTRY

Christian Helplines, Inc., and its member centers are engaged in Christian ministry. It is therefore required that Christian Helplines, Inc., and its member centers shall

1. Have a governing board whose members each have a declared commitment to Jesus Christ as personal Savior and Lord.

2. Have an Executive Director who has a declared commitment to Jesus Christ as personal Savior and Lord.

3. Have staff, volunteers, and telephone counselors, each of whom have a declared commitment to Jesus Christ as personal Savior and Lord.

4. Provide a minimum fifty-hour telephone counselor training program teaching:

(a) the principles of counseling in an accepting, nonjudgmental way following the example of Jesus Christ;

(b) the skill of active listening;

(c) the stages of counseling using the Christian Helplines, Inc., counseling model;

(d) the fundamentals of the Christian faith;

(e) how to pray with people, confront sinful behavior, and lead a caller into a personal relationship with Jesus Christ;

(f) the fundamentals of telephone counseling, crisis intervention, and making referrals; and

(g) the areas of primary caller concern (such as alcohol, loneliness, grief, divorce, marital problems, etc.) presenting specifically:

(1) background information   (3) biblical perspective
(2) counseling guidelines   (4) community resources

5. Offer twenty-four-hour-a-day telephone helpline services through approved telephone counselors at a centrally located counseling center.

6. Serve as an extension of the ministry of the local Christian church.

7. Obtain a Commissioning and Commitment Statement from each person associated with the member center (i.e., Board Members, Executive Director, Staff, Volunteers, Telephone Counselors).

COMISSIONING AND COMMITMENT STATEMENT

Dear Lord Jesus,
Thank You for calling me to serve You in this Helpline Ministry.

I acknowledge You as my personal Savior and Lord and ask that Your Holy Spirit fill me and teach me to listen and love as You do.

I pray that You will counsel and minister through me as together we reach out to those who are hurting in our community.

I promise to maintain the trust and confidence of all who call for help.

I promise to support the Helpline with my prayers, my service, and my gifts.

Appendix 3

Christian Telephone Counseling

The telephone was invented by Alexander Graham Bell in 1876. Today, this instrument has become a public utility that makes it possible for a person to talk almost instantly with people across town, across the country, and around the world.

As our world has changed, families and friends have come to live at great distances from each other. The telephone has become an essential part of our daily communication. Businesses and government have also come to depend on the telephone. It is, therefore, not surprising that the telephone has become the instrument around which an effective and unique ministry of personal counseling has evolved.

Over the years the Reverend Sir Alan Walker in Australia, the Reverend Dr. Ross E. Whetstone in the United States, and other visionary Christians have led the way in the development of the ministry of Christian telephone counseling. Helplines typically operate twenty-four hours a day, making it possible for anyone with any kind of problem to call at any hour of the day or night and be in touch with a trained Christian volunteer. Most telephone volunteers are laypeople who have received special training, although many pastors and professional counselors participate in these programs as well. Organizations such as Life Line International, CONTACT USA, The Samaritans, Tel-Care, and Christian Helplines, Inc., have been established to set standards of training and operations for telephone counseling, crisis intervention, information, and referral services around the world.

THE UNIQUENESS OF TELEPHONE COUNSELING

Telephone helplines are unique for several reasons.

Availability. One of the reasons for the success of telephone counseling is its availability. In much of the world, telephone communication is available to everyone, either through private or public means.

Accessibility. Telephone counselors make themselves available at all hours of the day and night. Helplines are open every day, never taking a holiday. Churches, counseling centers, and other offices offering help must close at day's end, and it often takes a while before an appointment can be arranged. Telephone counselors join together and commit themselves to always being accessible to the hurting people of the community.

Affordability. Professional help may be expensive and is often not essential. The free help extended by telephone counselors is, many times, all that is needed. People in crisis need someone they can talk with openly and honestly, someone who will listen and help them to think through their situation. Telephone counselors are trained to refer callers to professional counselors when the situation warrants.

Anonymity. Many times, people are afraid to let others know about their problems. Over the telephone, a person can remain anonymous. Often, a person will not talk to his pastor because he does not want his pastor to know about intimate personal problems. People are sometimes reluctant to turn to friends or family members for help until it is too late. Telephone counseling provides anonymity and allows people to seek help without revealing too much. Callers feel safe, secure, and in control. They can remain anonymous.

Acceptability. As a voice over the telephone, callers are accepted without regard to their appearance, weight, height, clothes, past behavior or reputation, age, race, religion, sex, social standing, or financial position. Some of these things may never be revealed to the telephone counselor. Prior knowledge of these things may predispose a person's attitude about the friend who comes seeking help. It is oftentimes easier to talk to a stranger than to someone you know. Not being able to see each other may make it easier as well.

Ability to Terminate. Finally, when a person reaches out for help over the telephone, he maintains control. He is able to hang up and terminate the call at any moment. Many times, a caller's life is out of control and being able to terminate the call helps to restore the caller's feeling of control. Having some control over his life is essential to his personal sanity, security, and peace of mind.

Telephone counseling is also limited in several ways. Not being able to physically be with a person has its limitations. After all, a lot can be communicated by body language:

- The way a person walks or sits in a chair
- His posture or facial expressions
- His personal grooming

- Eye contact, tears
- Cleanliness

The telephone counselor must, therefore, rely even more on a person's tone of voice, hesitations, sighing, shakiness, voice pitch, and other sounds that may reveal information about the caller.

Emergencies and Telephone Helping

Undoubtedly, the telephone is most helpful during emergencies. By using the telephone, help can be summoned quickly, without having to set up an appointment, travel to a meeting place, fill out forms, and wait. Telephone counseling and crisis intervention will often bypass or delay these barriers. The telephone is the most effective way to secure emergency assistance, such as police, fire, medical, or personal help. Most communities in the United States now provide a central calling number (911) for emergencies.

PROBLEM CALLERS

Chronic Caller

The chronic caller is a person who is emotionally stuck. He or she seldom wants to work on the problem or really change anything.

Chronic calls can be very draining on the emotions of telephone counselors. New counselors often become manipulated by these experienced chronic callers. Wanting so much to be of help, new counselors will be drawn into long weary telephone calls. Seasoned counselors may also become frustrated talking with "that same person who is going nowhere."

The important thing is for all counselors to recognize chronic callers by the fact that they tend to ramble on in conversation and not address any specific crisis or problem. When such a caller is recognized, the telephone counselor should be courteous and follow the counseling guidelines given in the Chronic Caller File. The counselor may need to confront the caller on his need to join organizations, clubs, and church to develop friendships; to continue in therapy, seek employment, etc., and then terminate the call. Case review guidelines are placed in helpline centers to give telephone counselors direction in handling specific chronic callers. The following guidelines will help to identify crisis callers vs. chronic callers.

Crisis Caller vs. Chronic Caller

Crisis Caller	Chronic Caller
1. Change There has been a recent significant change in the person's life, i.e., divorce, unemployment, argument with loved one.	**1. No Recent Change** Life just continues to grind away in the same old rut. No recent crisis event or change.
2. Time Frame Crisis goes through stages of shock, adjustment, and recovery. Movement is noted.	**2. No Time Frame** Extends on and on. Little change. Person stuck in crisis, no movement.
3. Focus Person can stay focused in discussion of crisis situation. Can determine sequence of events.	**3. No Focus** Conversation rambles. Difficult to determine sequence.
4. Desire Wants to change, receive help, work on solutions, make plans.	**4. No Desire** No desire to change. "Yes, but . . ." response to suggestions.

Counseling Guidelines

Step A

1. Read the Chronic Caller File and become familiar with the chronic callers.

2. Follow the contracts, guidelines, and time limits as stated.

3. If no guidelines or agreements are given, follow the general guidelines listed below in Step B.

Step B

1. Maintain control over the call. Do not let the person talk aimlessly without identifying a crisis/problem that he wants to focus on. Take control of the conversation. Do not wait for the caller to stop talking.

2. If the chronic caller simply wants to continue to discuss old problems, gently indicate your knowledge of these old problems and focus on what the caller has done to solve the problems. Focus on the caller's responsibility for changing the particular situation.

3. Ask for the specific reason he called at this time.

4. If a specific purpose for the call cannot be determined, remind the chronic caller that others in crisis may be trying to reach the helpline and terminate the call.

Telephone counselors should not feel guilty about hanging up on a chronic caller who just wants to visit and tie up the helpline. Phone lines must be kept open and free for crisis counseling and intervention callers. Follow the guidelines set down in the Chronic Caller File and keep the call short.

When chronic callers realize that helpline counselors are not just going to visit with them over the phone, they will call someplace else.

Silent Callers

It takes a lot of courage to reach out for help, yet some people find it difficult to speak once the telephone counselor has answered the phone. When this happens, counselors are encouraged to be patient and to stimulate conversation by saying something like the following:

"Sometimes, it's hard to talk." (pause)

"I want you to know that we care about you and we'd like to help you." (pause)

"You must really be hurting." (pause)

"Tell me what happened." (pause)

If there is no response, the telephone counselor might continue with:

"If you can't talk with me, I'm going to have to hang up." (pause)

"I'd really like to help." (pause)

"Call back later, when you feel you can talk. (pause) Goodbye." (pause) (hang up)

Sometimes the shock and trauma of a crisis is just too much for a person. The above dialogue attempts to draw the person out. But after a while, if the person does not talk, the telephone counselor must terminate the call.

Some chronic callers, who are angry because their call was terminated, may give the helpline counselor the "silent treatment." In either case, after a nurturing response, if the caller does not begin to respond, the call should be terminated.

Hang Ups

Chronic callers may hang up upon recognizing the telephone counselor's voice, realizing that the counselor is not going to play his "game" of allowing him to manipulate the line. Sexual callers, looking for a female to talk to, may hang up when a male answers the telephone.

Telephone counselors should not allow themselves to be badgered. If several hang ups or silent calls are received, take the phone off the hook and wait a short while (15 minutes) before activating the line again.

Sexual Callers

Do not allow conversations about sexual topics to become descriptive. It is simply not necessary to go into detail to understand a genuine sexual problem.

Do not respond to personal questions by callers who ask what you look like, what kind of clothing you are wearing, or other unnecessary personal inquiry. Be aware that some callers, especially males, will attempt to have sexual calls with female telephone counselors for the purpose of masturbation.

Telephone counselors need to be aware of their own feelings and emotions when counseling in sexual matters. Telephone counselors should feel free to ask callers to call back later and talk with another counselor, or to terminate an offensive or manipulative caller.

Obscene Caller

If you receive an obscene call, turn the hearing part of the telephone instrument to your forehead so you cannot hear what the caller is saying and speak into the mouthpiece of the phone. Pray aloud for the caller. For example:

"Heavenly Father, I lift up this man to You and ask that You convict him of his sin. Reveal the truth of Jesus Christ to him, and give him the faith to believe. Reveal Your love to him, oh God. Let him know that we love him. In the name of Jesus, I pray. Amen."

Check and see if he is still on the line. Try to draw him into a counseling call. If not interested, terminate the call. In all probability, he will have hung up. Obscene callers who are prayed over don't call back. The point is that the telephone counselor is not there to be abused. Do not listen to the obscenity.

Telephone Ministry

The telephone is one of the most common, and yet most effective means of personal communication in the world. For reasons expressed earlier, telephone ministry is very effective and efficient.

Telephone counseling can be used to give encouragement, support, information and referral, help in developing plans, providing guidance, and confronting destructive and sinful behavior. Telephone counseling is tremendously effective in reaching people who are outside of the church and those who do not have a personal relationship with Jesus Christ and His Holy Spirit. People who are grieving, people who are in crisis, going through a divorce, having marital problems, teenagers, shut-ins, handicapped persons, people who cannot afford professional counseling, or people who do not feel comfortable talking about personal problems with their pastor, people who need prayer, and people who just need someone to talk to at any hour of the day or night, all find that telephone counseling can help meet their needs.

For more information on starting a Christian helpline in your community, contact Christian Helplines, Inc., at

CHRISTIAN HELPLINES, INC.
P.O. BOX 10855
TAMPA, FLORIDA 33679
TELEPHONE (813) 874-5509

About the Author

Dr. William H. "Skip" Hunt received a bachelor degree in business administration from the University of Georgia, with special training in public securities and private business development. In his thirties, he served as vice president of two mutual funds, national sales manager of a fifty-million-dollar investment company, and as a partner in a member firm of the New York Stock Exchange. Skip was later co-founder and president of Family Television Corporation, owner and operator of WFTS TV-28, in Tampa, Florida.

In spite of his business success and happy marriage with two children, Skip's life was void of real meaning until he met Jesus on March 23, 1975. His life has not been the same since.

Skip became founder and board chairman of Christian Helplines, Inc., a nationwide network of local crisis helpline centers. He also pursued and obtained a master's in Christian counseling and a doctor of philosophy in psychology at Faith Theological Seminary in Tampa, Florida.

Skip welcomes personal correspondence at

CHRISTIAN HELPLINES, INC.
P.O. Box 10855
Tampa, FL 33679